Professional Power
Personal Excellence

Professional Power Personal Excellence

7 Integrated Steps to Accelerate Your Career!

Gary K. Yamamoto, Ph.D.

Cypress Mountain Books
Tucson

To my wife for all her inspiration and support

CYPRESS MOUNTAIN BOOKS
An Imprint of Dynamic Pathways, Inc.
Tucson, Arizona

International Standard Book Number: 1-878182-14-5

Library of Congress Catalog Card Number: 96-84921

10 9 8 7 6 5 4 3 2 1

Printed in the United States of America

Table of Contents

Preface

As we step deeper into the Information Age, the rate of change accelerates and transforms our familiar world into a cyber world. Organizations that succeed in this rapidly evolving environment must be flexible, capable of responding rapidly to the constantly changing demands of its customers.

To become more flexible, organizations have been moving towards the virtual organization. In such an organization, people are employed only because of the "value" they bring to that organization. They may be hired to complete specific tasks or projects. Or else, they may be hired because of a special talent and/or skill they possess. When the task or project is completed, or they no longer meet the needs of that organization, they are then relocated within the organization or terminated.

To excel in this unpredictable environment, you need an effective strategy to constantly increase your value to an organization. Regardless of your position, you have to have a clear pathway, a step-by-step process to guide your professional development. *You must become accountable to yourself, and learn how to take control and create your own future.*

This book provides you with a seven-step road map that will allow you to take control of your professional career — and your personal life. Each of the seven steps will help you to improve your professional performance and productivity. It will provide you with the principles for using all of your natural talents and abilities. In addition, it will teach you how to balance your life so that your professional success is not achieved at the price of your personal life. Here's a brief summary of what you will find in this book:

Step 1 (Work Hard) shows you how to maintain the right skills to do your job and how to keep yourself motivated. This is the basic performance level desired by employers, and it makes you a valuable worker. Yet, if you are to excel, more is required.

In Step 2 (Work Smart), you will learn how to upgrade your knowledge base quickly and easily. However, for knowledge to become useful, you must learn how to communicate effectively.

Step 3 (Think Smart) shows you how to prepare yourself and create your future. You will learn how to overcome the limitations of your beliefs and habits, master the process of change, and create the life you desire.

Step 4 (Lead) helps you identify your vision and focus your activities on achieving that vision. Leadership also requires the ability to develop teamwork, support, and, ultimately, synergy.

Step 5 (Innovate) teaches you how to tap your native creativity and unleash innovative ideas and solutions. Only through constant innovation is it possible to develop unique products, services, marketing ideas, and sales techniques to outperform the competition. Also required at this step is the ability to maintain a positive state of being which inspires others and also helps you to handle difficulties and setbacks.

Step 6 (Personal Best) teaches you the power of high ethics, values, and right character in your life. These are important in creating the right organizational culture, gaining the trust of customers and fellow workers, and enhancing your own personal integrity.

Finally, Step 7 (Balance) enables you to truly balance your professional life with your personal life and enjoy both more fully.

This practical book provides you with powerful tools for mastering your life. It can help you transform your life, regain your professional power and excellence, and fully enjoy your life once more, or perhaps for the first time! Good luck and let's get going!

Gary K. Yamamoto
Tucson, Arizona
1996

Chapter 1
Creating a Change

If you are not willing to change your life, someone else will do it for you.
— Gary K. Yamamoto

We are living at the dawning of the Information Age. In it, information is being created at an ever-increasing rate. Nevertheless, the real power of this age does not lie in information. For information to become useful, the knowledge contained within the information must be extracted.

However, knowledge alone is still not the real power. The real power lies in your ability to apply that knowledge. The application of knowledge is called wisdom. Thus the real power of the Information Age lies within your mind. The human mind is not only the most important power within each of us, it is also the most unused.

You, like everyone else, were born with a mind full of unlimited potential. Unfortunately, somewhere along your journey through life, you gave away that infinite potential to become "just human."

Like you, I did exactly the same thing. My inability to understand how my mind functioned and how to really improve my life led me down a slow ever-descending path. I was caught like a rat in a circular maze, going nowhere.

Life had become a mad rush of events that consumed all my time. There were the constant demands of work, along with the strain of raising three stepchildren. Then there was my ensuing divorce and the problems it created. My life had become a blur as I rushed to complete one thing after another. My obligations left me feeling physically tired and mentally drained. Yet the faster I did things, the less time I seemed to have, and the more quickly the months and years flew past me.

Creating a Change

When the futility of my past actions had become apparent, I decided to take some kind of action. I knew that if the results were going to change, I would have to do something different. Fortunately, there were only three basic things I could change in my life. I could change my environment, other people, or myself.

Changing Our Environment

One option was to change my environment. If my job felt uncomfortable, I could get a new position or job. If my relationship seemed less than fulfilling, I could get a separation or a divorce and then find a new relationship.

Yet, I knew that this would not result in a permanent solution. Like you, I have watched what happens to people who move from job to job, relationship to relationship. I have seen them move into new homes, purchase new cars, go shopping, or redecorate their homes. In the end, the results are usually the same. Although changes seem to improve their lives, the results are seldom permanent. In time, and often in a very short time, they are looking for another environmental change.

Have you observed this happening, either in yourself or in your friends and acquaintances? You may know people who have shifted from one job to another. When they first begin a new job, everything seems "great" and they appear to be happy again. But in short order, they begin having similar problems with management or co-workers. Predictably, the situation soon becomes too difficult to tolerate and they rush off again, creating yet another environmental change.

In their personal lives, they rush from one relationship to another. When they find the "perfect" person, everything seems rosy. Unfortunately, they cannot see what everyone else sees: that the new person is a near clone of the former one. In time, the relationship deteriorates and the problems return. These unhappy people again rush off in search of the perfect relationship.

If you find yourself identifying with this situation, it is time to get off that track! Let us investigate the next possibility, that of changing others.

Changing Other People

Trying to force other people to change is a popular option. Unfortunately, this is one of the most difficult, and often unrewarding, tasks you can ever undertake. Every administrator, manager, parent, and teacher has experienced this. Fortunately there are effective methods to entice other people to change, and we will discuss these later in this book. For now, you should be aware that there is no effective way to *force* other people to change.

People resist your efforts to change them because for them to change would be an admission of error. No one likes to admit that he or she was wrong. Trying to force others to change meets with automatic resistance, even when the change promises to help them. The more you push, the harder they fight back. If you push too hard, they may strike back or leave. In the end, you simply wear yourself out, possibly creating a lot of bad feelings and even a few enemies in the process.

Changing Ourselves

Henry David Thoreau said, "Things do not change; we change." Changing yourself may be the change of last resort, but it is also the best and most effective type of change you can choose.

When you look back into your life, you will see that your attempts to change yourself have met with varying degrees of success. A few changes may have been easy for you, but there were always those changes that were very difficult. Despite months and even years of struggle, you may have found yourself falling back to where you originally were. Like most people, you have found some areas in which it was nearly impossible to create a significant and long-lasting change.

Being able to change yourself is the key to professional power and personal excellence. In the next chapter, we discuss how you can accelerate your career by increasing your productivity and, ultimately, your value to your organization.

Chapter 2

In Search of Professional Power, Personal Excellence

You can take away all my capital assets, and I will be wealthy in two years. But if you take away my people, all is lost. — Andrew Carnegie

My wife and I had just heard a technology expert describe the latest breakthroughs that would increase individual productivity. He cited the latest inventions that were going to play a key role in creating the future.

"What do you think about what we heard tonight?" my wife asked.

"Technology's great," I answered. "But it won't give any company an edge over anyone else."

"Why not?"

"Well . . ." I began slowly, as I secretly stepped onto my soapbox, "companies think that if they have the latest technology, they will have a great advantage over their competitors. So they rush out and buy all the latest equipment and systems. But as soon as they purchase the new equipment, they are faced with a couple of problems."

"What kind of problems?"

"For one thing, some of their people may have a resistance to using the new technology. Their reluctance to learn how to operate the new system may actually slow them down. Then there are those people who find it impossible to adapt to the new equipment. The company has to replace these people with new people, which is expensive.

"And then of course, the same salesperson who sold them the new technology is also hustling to sell the same system to their competitors. In a very short time, any technological edge they may have had will disappear. Not only that, their competitors may have already purchased the next generation of equipment which outperforms their system. Then their technological advantage becomes a liability and they have to update their equipment again."

"So how does an organization gain an advantage over the competition?" my wife asked.

"The real advantage is in their people," I said excitedly, with my hands expressing my enthusiasm. I was feeling hot now. "People are the key, but only if management can help them to do their best. Every single person already knows how to improve his or her performance by at least 10 percent. This additional performance goes directly to the bottom line. A 10 percent improvement may double the profits in some companies. Management's job is to guide their people to unleash this hidden potential and increase their performance by . . ."

"Are you practicing another of your speeches?" interrupted my wife.

I laughed and quietly stepped off my soapbox. She had probably heard this from me before. She understood my position that the key to productivity is people. When people are given the right tools and treated properly, they can excel. For you to excel, you must develop an effective step-by-step improvement strategy.

Productivity

The productivity of any organization or individual is dependent on two factors and can be written as follows:

Productivity = System Efficiency x Individual Performance

System efficiency is the combined efficiency of all the equipment and operating processes in an organization. It includes computer systems, machinery, and operating procedures. Organizations spend a lot of money and time trying to maximize their system efficiency as a strategic advantage against competitors. Unfortunately, most of their competitors have a similar system efficiency.

The real key to productivity is found in individual performance, in the individuals who operate the equipment and use the operating procedures. When people are taught properly and feel motivated to work, they work more efficiently and effectively. As individual performance rises, bottom-line productivity increases dramatically. The rest of this book shows you how to improve your performance, which will, in turn, accelerate your career.

Performance

Individual performance is also made up of two factors: a person's ability and his or her behavior. The relationship can be written as follows:

Individual Performance = Ability x Behavior

To achieve excellence, you must excel in both of these areas — ability and behavior. It makes little difference what type of work you do. If you are able to excel in both of these areas, you will naturally increase your performance and productivity. The interrelationship between these two factors determines productivity and can be illustrated as shown in the following figure:

BEHAVIOR	Low ABILITY	High ABILITY
High	Gopher	Master
Low	Bureaucrat	Philosopher

Figure 2-1: Individual Performance

When a person has low ability and his or her behavior is minimal, we have the classic definition of a bureaucrat. Bureaucrats have little ability to do their jobs and they accomplish very little *real* productive work. Essentially they occupy a slot on the organizational chart or warm a chair in an office. It never fails that when people hear my description of a bureaucrat, they immediately chuckle and are reminded of some sloth in the organization.

Suppose, miracles of miracles, that a bureaucrat suddenly decides to move out of character and increase his or her ability. The person goes to school and learns a lot about his or her job. With high ability and low motivation, the bureaucrat has now moved over to the classic definition of a philosopher.

Philosophers are long on ideas but short on muscle. They possess tremendous knowledge and capabilities. They can easily solve almost any problem. However, as long as their behavior remains low and lacks follow-through, they fail to capitalize on their great knowledge. As a general rule, philosophers think and talk a lot but rarely accomplish much.

On the other hand, suppose that a bureaucrat somehow becomes motivated. He or she is now ready and willing to do anything. We generally call these people "gophers." Gophers have absolutely no idea of what to do or when to do it. They behave like big, eager robots, awaiting any order to charge forth and take action. Although they are wonderful workers and willing to do almost anything, they need constant guidance and supervision. To survive, gophers often find themselves associated with and taking orders from philosophers.

Gophers are often new hires in an organization. Unless they are given the right training and education, they eventually lose their enthusiasm. In a very short time, a gopher slips down to become just another bureaucrat.

The final category consists of people who have both the right ability and the right behavior. These people are the true masters of life. Masters are able to upgrade their abilities constantly to meet the changing demands of their professions. They can motivate themselves, doing whatever is necessary to accomplish the task at hand. They also tend to rise to the top of their professions. People in the "master" category are the ones who definitely exhibit professional power and personal excellence.

Seven Steps

To help you balance and master your career and life, I have identified seven integrated steps that you must attain. This seven-step program is a systematic strategy for attaining professional power and personal excellence. The first five steps are primarily concerned with your professional development, although they can also be focused on your personal development. The last two steps primarily guide your personal development. Figure 2-2 illustrates the seven steps and how they are related to each other.

The following is a quick overview of how the seven steps can help you to gain professional power and personal excellence.

Step 1: Work Hard

Ability = Skill

Behavior = Motivation

Every job requires certain basic skills, the hands-on "how to" ability to do the job. When hiring people, management and personnel departments always try to hire people who have the right skills. You must have the right skills to get a job. To hold onto the job, you must constantly upgrade your skills.

Your skills are not sufficient unless you are motivated to apply them. Because there will always be a job for a hard worker who has the right skills and is self-motivated, you must maintain your motivation under all conditions.

Step 2: Work Smart

Ability = Knowledge

Behavior = Communication

To work smart, you must gain a wider knowledge of your job. You must not only know your job better, but also gain in-depth and useful information on a number of job-related subjects. With knowledge, you now understand "why" things occur, and you will tend to manage those who know only "how" things are accomplished.

Knowledge in itself is not useful until it is communicated. Effective communication transmits more than facts. It projects feelings and emotions to give people a real sense of what you are trying to communicate.

Step 3: Think Smart

Ability = Beliefs

Behavior = Habits

This step assists you in creating permanent changes. Your ability to change is usually limited by your present beliefs and habits. You

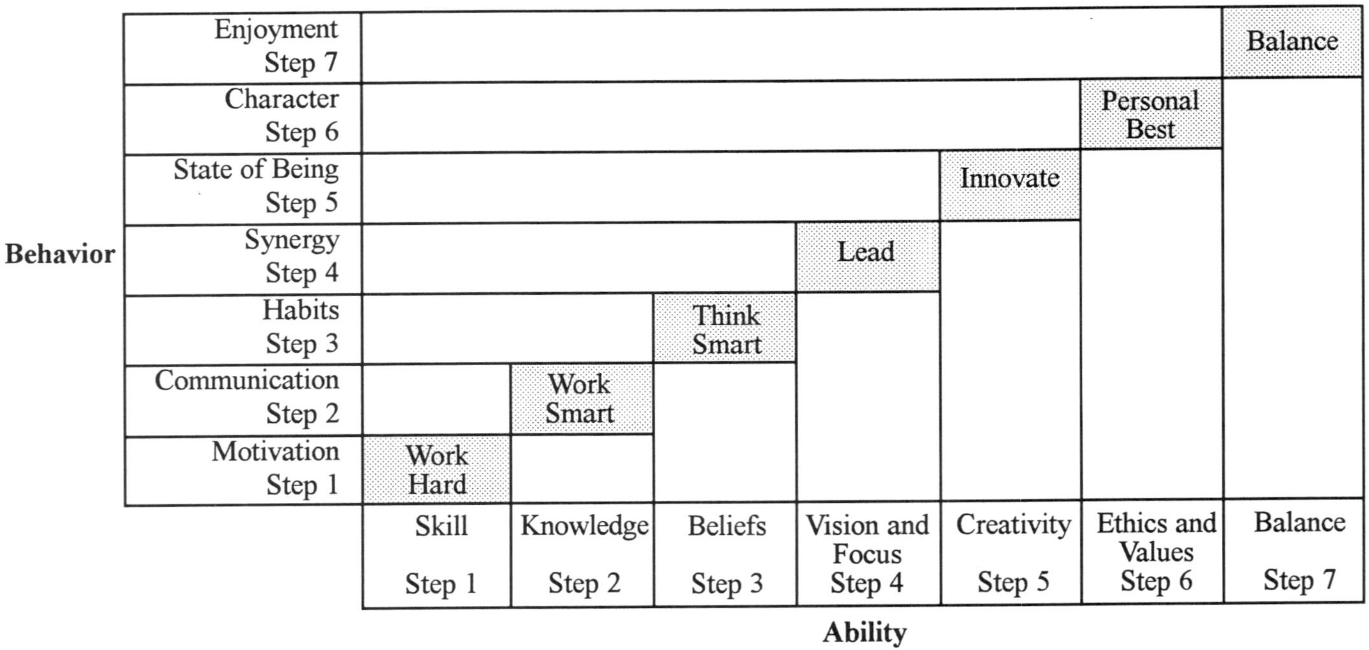

Figure 2-2: The Seven Steps of Professional Power, Personal Excellence

will learn how to make significant and simultaneous changes to both your beliefs and habits to create profound changes in your life.

Step 4: Lead

Ability = Vision and Focus

Behavior = Synergy

Leadership requires a powerful vision to guide your effort and the effort of others. Along with vision, you must develop the ability to focus your energies and the energies of others to achieve your vision.

A powerful vision is best achieved through teamwork, but simply having people work together is not enough. To rise to peak performance levels, synergy is desired. Exceptional leaders motivate their people to operate from this level, rise to peak performance levels, and exceed all expectations.

Step 5: Innovate

Ability = Creativity

Behavior = State of Being

Step 5 allows you to move beyond your limiting paradigms. By understanding how your mind functions, you can move beyond the limits of thinking and tap your creative mind. Creativity is the key to developing innovative products, services, marketing ideas, customer service, and sales.

This step also requires a positive state of being to influence others. A positive state of being allows you to guide the efforts of others, while you mentally transform your job and life, making them much more enjoyable.

Step 6: Personal Best

Ability = Ethics and Values

Behavior = Character

Ethics and right values are also essential to your success. In business, your ethics and values determine the path you choose and influence how your clients and prospects perceive you. Additionally, living your ethics and values brings you peace of mind because you have done the "right" thing.

Your character determines how you perform under various conditions. This is especially true when you are under pressure. In Step 6, you will learn how to live your ethics and values, and excel.

Step 7: Balance

Ability = Balance

Behavior = Enjoyment

Balance is the final key to the seven steps. People usually succeed in one area of life at the expense of other areas. True success demands a balance between your professional life and your personal life. Mastering this level teaches you to enjoy the whole of life, not to just snatch a few specific moments of fun. After all, what good is the attainment of all that life has to offer if neither you nor your loved ones enjoy the journey?

Time to Begin

This book is structured to move you from Step 1 up to Step 7. *Each of the seven steps is broken down into two parts — ability and behavior.* You can also create your own personal strategy by choosing a step that you wish to develop. Select any step you may have bypassed in your career or life, and then choose to work on it.

To truly excel, you must master all seven steps. The more steps you master, the closer you will be to attaining professional power and personal excellence. Mastery is definitely within your grasp. The following chapters provide you with effective strategies and methods to transform your life. You can accelerate your career, regain your power, achieve excellence, enjoy life more, and fulfill your true potential.

Step 1
Work Hard
(ability)

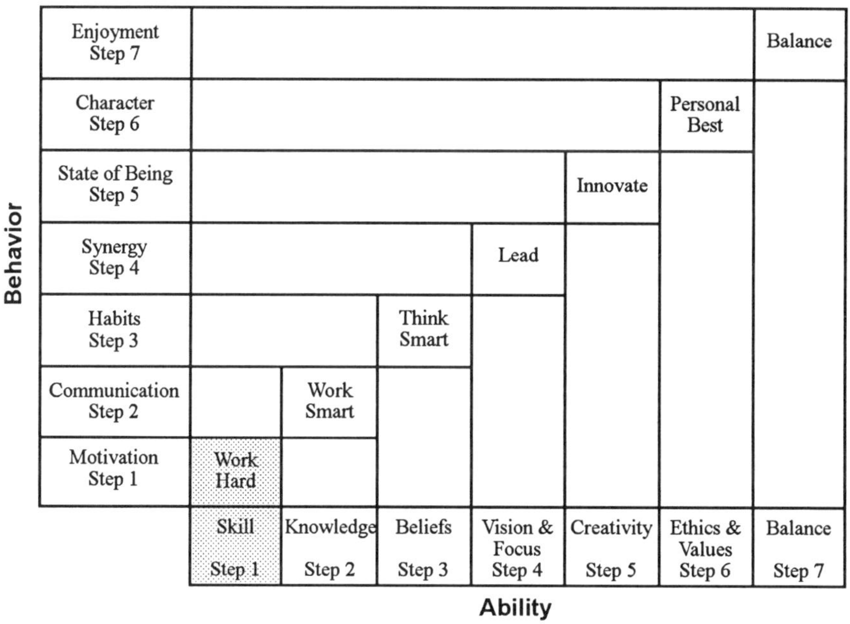

Chapter 3

Step 1: Work Hard (ability)

Skill: Constant Improvement

If you're not getting any better, you're probably getting worse.

— Gary K. Yamamoto

Before we dive into adventurous and new concepts, let us start with some basics, some of which you already know. Every job and career requires that you possess and maintain certain basic skills. Your skills are a collection of basic "how to" information that allows you to complete successfully the tasks required by your job. The more skillful you are, the better you are able to accomplish your job. To remain current with changing times, you must constantly upgrade your skills.

Management and human resources personnel are constantly on the lookout for people who have the right skills. Organizations hire people who have demonstrated mastery of their ability to accomplish the tasks that define a particular job. The better you are at doing a job, the greater your chances to obtain and hold onto that job.

Each position requires a surprising number of skills. For instance, salespeople must have basic sales skills. Under the umbrella of selling, they need efficient prospecting methods, riveting presentations, and effective closing techniques. However, even these are not enough.

In today's competitive and sophisticated marketplace, customers demand more. To meet this growing demand, salespeople must also exhibit effective communication and provide great customer service. In mastering prospecting, they must also be effective networkers and become efficient in computer database management. Finally, they must have the necessary insight to uncover the prospect's real problems and proactively offer practical solutions to address those problems.

As you can see, a salesperson can no longer survive with basic selling skills. Every salesperson needs a variety of skills to deal with a more technologically sophisticated work environment, a more competitive sales arena, and a more demanding universe of prospects and customers.

What is true for a salesperson is also true for you. You can enhance your value to your employer by increasing the number of skills you possess. The more skills you learn, the more valuable you become to your employer.

Additional skills are relatively easy to obtain. You can receive informal cross-training by working with another person in a related job, or you can attend a formal seminar or training session to learn new skills.

Most of the training provided by companies to employees teaches them more skills. The more skills you have, the more effective you are in your job or career. Additional skills make you better qualified to serve your clients. The bottom-line result of gaining additional skills is that you become more effective and productive, have greater job security, obtain more referrals, and gain repeat business.

Preparing for the Future

In an environment of rapid change, you should never feel too secure in your work situation. Are you really indispensable? A lot of people thought they were until the downsizing bandwagon changed that perception. No matter how skillful you are, a quick change in consumer needs or a shift in corporate direction could send your job or career to the "graveyard."

New technology makes people obsolete. The best switchboard operator in the world became obsolete with an office messaging system. Middle managers are being eliminated as computer systems extract useful information from data, identify trends, and simplify upper-management decisions.

Competition can take away your job. Even the best pineapple picker in Hawaii is now out of a job because the foreign producers have made it uneconomical to grow pineapples commercially in Hawaii.

In an environment of constant organizational changes, such as downsizing, right-sizing, corporate mergers, and so on, you may find yourself out of a job. Technology may make your skills useless and no longer marketable. Remember, *"If you are not moving ahead, you are falling behind."* When your skills become obsolete, you may be shown the door marked "exit only." To make yourself more valuable, you must prepare for the future. Ask yourself the following questions:

- Am I preparing myself for my next job or career?
- Have I identified the new skills I need in order to obtain my next job?
- Have I really committed myself to learning a new skill?
- Have I backed my desires with the necessary funds and time to upgrade my skills?
- Am I really committed to getting more training?

Surveys indicate that a person stays in a job or position for an average of five years. About every five years, people leave their jobs for one reason or another. Be kind to yourself and prepare for this. Expect that your new job or position may require new skills, a drastic upgrade, or a change in the skills you already possess.

Your Next Career

Statistically, the average person now entering the workforce can expect to have five different careers. Prepare yourself by expecting to have a different career soon. Never allow yourself to be put into a position in which you lose your job and then say, "I didn't think they were going to get rid of my job. I'm not prepared for the future. I need to be trained for another job. I want the government or my old company to pay me to get the necessary training for another job."

In most cases, changes do not occur overnight. They usually come in visible phases, and you will almost always see them coming. After all, this is the Information Age! With all the information available, it is almost impossible not to detect an impending change. Your problem is not that you fail to see the change coming, but that you mistakenly assume that you, personally, will not be affected. Or you might play the ostrich game, not willing to acknowledge the impending change or else praying that the situation will pass you by.

In my personal life, I have had three separate and completely different careers. I have been an electronics engineer and manager, and the co-owner and CEO of a publishing company. Now I am the president of a professional speaking and management consulting firm. As a professional speaker, I am constantly upgrading my presentation skills and the content of my materials. Just recently I switched from the use of overheads in my presentations to a multimedia presentation system. I am using a state-of-the-art laptop computer with a new presentation software program to obtain the top-notch, cutting-edge results I desire.

Nevertheless, I would not be upset if I had to embark on another career. Being an active member of the National Speakers Association and a board member of the Arizona Chapter, I attend their conferences and meetings regularly to upgrade my speaking skills. At a minimum, I read at least two new books a month and listen to a number of audiotapes. By constantly upgrading my skills, I feel I am prepared to meet most of the changes that life can throw my way. What do you do to keep yourself on the cutting edge of your job or profession? If the answer is "nothing," you must begin now!

Upgrading Skills

Skills are quite easy to upgrade. New skills are just as easy to obtain. You simply need to commit yourself to the task and receive more training. Then you have to locate an appropriate training course and actually take it.

There are many different avenues for upgrading your skills in every conceivable subject, including sales, management, negotiations, customer service, computers, and software programs. The following are a few sources:

- Books
- Audiocassette courses
- Videocassette courses
- Computer software and CDs
- Community college training courses

- Seminar training companies
- In-house cross-training

Unfortunately, there will always be those who are not interested in really upgrading their skills. They are content with maintaining the status quo, a minimum skill level that lets them keep their present jobs. Others are satisfied with maintaining an adequate skill level that makes them competent to do their jobs. They seem content with taking an occasional training seminar, but only if it is required and funded by their employer. Otherwise, they have little interest.

Maintaining a minimal skill level is acceptable only in a static environment. The last static environment occurred during our great-grandparents' lifetime, at the beginning of the twentieth century. *In today's rapidly changing and evolving world, standing still for even a short period of time could prove to be fatal!*

Training

According to a recent ASTD (American Society of Training and Development) survey of 15,000 large and medium-sized companies, only 0.5 percent of these organizations accounted for 90 percent of all the training dollars spent. Most corporations are not interested in training their people. Many seem to be in the business of using people and then getting rid of them. They hire skill and exploit it. When the skill is no longer useful, they cast the person out.

A few of you may be lucky enough to work for one of the few organizations committed to providing people with training. The rest of you, the vast majority, cannot afford to wait. You must take responsibility and action in order to prepare yourself.

Are you preparing yourself for your future? You can test yourself by simply asking the following questions:

- In the past month, what have I learned to make myself more valuable to my employer?
- What will I learn this month that makes me better at my job?
- What new skill or skills do I now possess that I did not have a year ago?
- Have I made my new skill or skills evident to my employer?

If you find little or nothing on the list, you are not doing very well. In fact, you are steadily falling behind and getting worse. Remember, as your environment changes (and it is changing rapidly), standing still means that you are falling behind. You must stop relying on your employer, who may not be interested in, or in the position of, giving you any new skill training. *You must become accountable for your own future.*

I recently had a problem with my plumbing, so I called in a plumber. Frank arrived and began testing my systems. Middle-aged at most, Frank seemed to be enjoying himself as he worked efficiently. He appeared so good at his job that I jokingly asked him if he had forty years of training on the job.

He smiled and replied, "Almost. I've been doing plumbing since I was seven. As a kid, I used to help this plumber in my neighborhood. He was the one who really got me started."

As we talked, I realized that here was a man who really loved his job. He sincerely looked forward to going to work and did not mind working hard. What I really admired was his attitude. He was just so positive. Curious, I asked him,

"Frank, what do you really like about working?"

"Oh," he chuckled, "I look forward to learning something new every day. If I didn't learn anything new, this job would get really boring."

"I'll bet," I agreed. "Not too much has changed in plumbing, has it?"

"No, not too much," he laughed. "That's why learning something new is a real challenge. When I learn something new, it makes me better."

We talked a little as he worked. I learned a little bit more about my toilets, and he learned a little bit about electrical systems. I thanked him for sharing his skills, and he thanked me for sharing mine. A fair trade, I would say.

Now, if Frank, with his generally routine work tasks, can challenge himself to learn something new every day, you can surely do the same. He works to upgrade himself every single day.

You must commit both the time and the funds to upgrade your skills. When you have committed yourself, go out and actually do it. One of the joys of upgrading your skills is that the process never ends.

Each new skill will suggest more skills you can learn. Life transforms itself into an adventure of discovering how you can excel beyond your present capabilities.

How do you decide which new skill you should learn? Begin by surveying your job or your personal life. Ask yourself the following questions:

- What skill, if I had it now, would make me more valuable at work?
- What skill would make my work more enjoyable?
- What skill would make me a better person with whom to work or live?

The answer is usually obvious. If not, ask a co-worker, a friend, your boss, or a family member. You may then discover that what you must do is exactly what you have been resisting all along.

For instance, many people find that they lack basic computer skills. They have probably known for a long time that learning how to use a computer would greatly improve their employment and promotion potential. Unfortunately, they have been dragging their feet and giving themselves a lot of excuses as to why they just cannot do it. If you find yourself in that position, take action now! Give yourself the training necessary to upgrade your skills.

Improving Through Practice

After you have learned a new skill, you have to practice it. Like any skill, if you don't use it, it quickly disappears. The old saying, "Use it or lose it," still applies, so practice those new skills every day. The more you practice, the faster you improve. All athletes know this, as it pertains to sports. You can extend the concept of regular practice to your professional skills. When you learn a new skill, practice it often, perhaps a dozen times a day. If you do this, you will have completed sixty practice sessions by the end of the week. In a year, you will have done it more than three thousand times.

A skillful person always has a job, but to achieve levels of excellence, you need more. You must utilize your skills effectively. You have to know how to motivate yourself, the right "behavior" attribute of Step 1.

Step 1
Work Hard
(behavior)

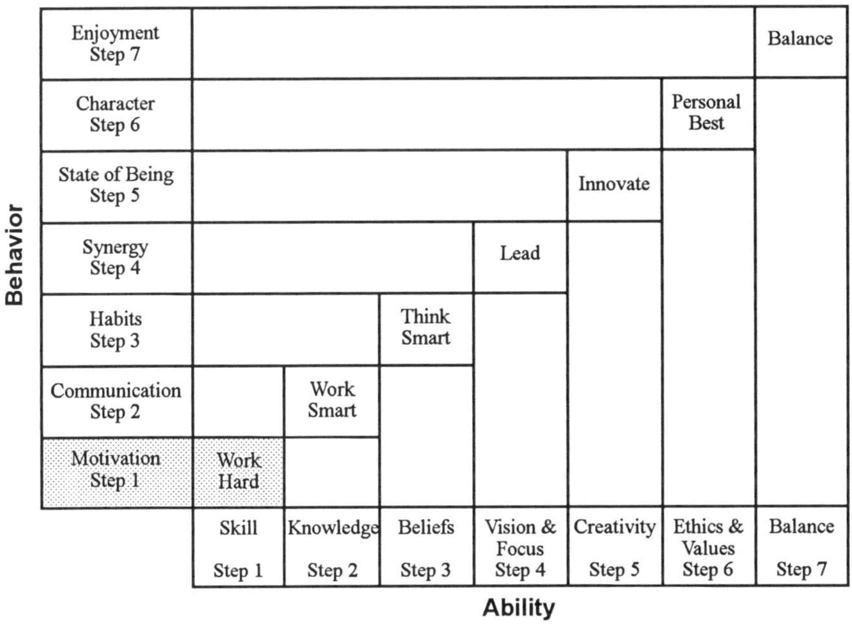

Chapter 4
Step 1: Work Hard (behavior)
Motivation: Self-Motivation

It is well-recognized that the highly motivated person succeeds in life. All successful people are motivated people.
— Henry Cannon

Having great skills is simply not enough. To stand out in a world full of skillful people, you also have to take action and obtain results. Nothing is accomplished until you motivate yourself to act.

Unfortunately, a lot of people refuse to take responsibility for their own motivation. They feel it is management's job to motivate them into action. Because of this attitude, they seem to naturally gravitate toward an apathetic state. They seem to be happy and content just sitting back and doing as little as possible, or doing what they have always been doing. I call these states "inertia" and "momentum."

Inertia and Momentum

The state of inertia is a physics principle whereby an object tends to remain at rest until a force is applied, causing it to move. In other words, a rock on the ground has inertia. It is not going to get up and move by itself. When a force is applied to the rock, it resists the force. Only when the force is large enough to overcome the rock's inertia will the rock finally move.

In the same manner, a lot of people live a portion of their lives in a state of constant inertia. They have a tendency to do nothing at all. When a force is applied to them, they automatically resist the force. Only when the force is great enough will they finally move into action.

We can see this in people's "not my job" attitude. They may see something that needs to be done, but it is not their direct responsibility. Even if it is a simple job that will only take a few minutes, they sit back and do nothing. In this particular area, they are in inertia.

Momentum is another physics principle. It means that an object in motion continues to move in the same direction until a force is applied to change its direction. A lot of people tend to have tremendous momentum. In the workplace, momentum can be equated to the "I've always done it this way" syndrome. People with momentum advise others with momentum-supporting comments, such as, "Don't rock the boat," "Just do your job," or "This is our standard procedure." When people are in momentum, they simply keep on doing the same old thing, over and over, day after day.

Like everyone else, you have this tendency to remain in inertia and momentum. You may identify this tendency by using many different names or phrases, such as laziness, cruising, or "That's just the way I am." *But if you want to create a change in your life, you have to overcome your own inertia and momentum.* Unfortunately, inertia and momentum are difficult to overcome.

The Power of Inertia and Momentum

Opportunities to create change are constantly coming your way. If you live in the states of momentum and inertia, you will automatically resist all attempts to change. You will tend to reject the idea first, then mentally support your negative decision with reasons and excuses.

For instance, suppose that a person named John sees that his situation at work is getting worse. He begins to think of what he can do to prepare himself for the future. He develops a few ideas and a plan of action.

Unfortunately, John's tendency to maintain momentum and inertia will immediately try to reject his plan. He begins talking to himself as follows:

"You know, I don't think anything's going to happen. Besides, it's too much work and takes too much energy to do everything in the plan. Maybe I should wait a few more days. Things will probably get better by then. After all, things have always worked out in the past. It's probably going to be the same this time. I'll just wait and see."

If John listens to his self-talk, he will procrastinate. He may continue to *think* about doing something. He may even talk about it to others. But in the end, he will probably *do* nothing at all.

Now suppose that a great opportunity comes John's way. Further suppose that this opportunity would increase his income by 10 percent. His new position would require less travel so he could spend more time with his family. But just as John did in the first scenario, he again thinks about making a change. Once again John will begin talking to himself:

"Hey, what am I really getting into? I mean, I really don't know whether I have what it takes to succeed. The job will probably require a lot of things that I don't know how to do.

"Oh, remember what happened to Fred? He made the same kind of change and couldn't cut it. Fred just couldn't meet their high standards and ended up getting demoted. People were snickering behind his back. Those standards are really high. What if I don't measure up? What if I fail, just like Fred did?

"Then what will people think? They'll be saying the same things they are now saying about Fred. What will my wife say? What will the kids think? Oh, and I can hear my in-laws now! I think it's probably best if I wait for an even better opportunity. There's probably something easier out there, or maybe even something with more pay.

"I think I should just wait before I apply for this job. A few days won't hurt. Besides, it will give me time to clarify what I really want to do."

If John listens to his self-chatter, he will probably not take any action. Another opportunity will have passed him by. He will again remain where he currently is, a victim of his own momentum and inertia.

As unfortunate as it sounds, a lot of people are just like John. They have a tendency to resist change, even when the pain gets bad and the future possibilities are really good. They almost naturally seem to choose not to take any action. They wait for the perfect time or opportunity before they finally act. For most, that time to take action never comes.

The famous Green Bay Packers coach, Vince Lombardi, once said, "Every coach knows about the same plays, the only difference is my ability to motivate people."

All of the other coaches knew the same plays that Vince Lombardi did. Athletes that played for the other teams had about the same talent as his players did. What was Vince Lombardi's secret? It was his ability to excite people and build enthusiasm.

The difference in talent between professionals in the same field is not that great. Professionals in any field have about the same skills and knowledge, differing by only a few percentage points. But the difference in individual motivation is tremendous. It may be hundreds or even thousands of percentage points. The difference in the results motivated people achieve is substantial.

If you want to achieve professional power and personal excellence, you must overcome your own inertia and momentum. Do not sabotage yourself. Learn what factors affect your enthusiasm and how you can motivate yourself.

Motivators of Change

I have found that there are only three factors that can motivate a person to create a change: pain, pleasure, and the price (amount of effort) it takes to accomplish the change. In the old days, these motivators were called the "stick," the "carrot," and the "work" it took to create the change. Today, they are better known as "punishment," "incentive," and "effort." Whatever they are called, the bottom line to motivation still involves pain, pleasure, and price of change.

There is a basic difference in how pain and pleasure motivate people. When pain is used, people are usually motivated to move away from it. They take all kinds of action to avoid, escape, reduce, or remove the pain. The greater the pain, the greater their incentive to avoid the pain.

On the other hand, people are generally motivated toward pleasure or the promise of pleasure. The greater the pleasure, the stronger their attraction to that pleasure. The greater the probability that they will receive that pleasure, the greater their motivation.

To further understand how pain and pleasure personally motivate you, let me introduce my concept of "here" and "there." "Here" generically represents where you are right now. "There" represents where you actually want to go and is illustrated in figure 4-1.

In general, if "here" is pleasurable, you have a tendency to remain "here." No one wants to change a pleasurable life. It is only after

Here → There

Figure 4-1: Change

"here" starts to become unpleasant or painful that you become motivated to move. The greater the pain, the more motivated you are to leave.

On the other hand, you will not move toward "there" if "there" promises to be more painful. Only if "there" promises to provide less pain or more pleasure will you become motivated to move toward "there." In general, the greater the pain "here," and the greater the pleasure "there," the more motivated you are to leave "here" and arrive "there."

Price of Change

For every change you attempt, there is a price you have to pay. The price you pay is the amount of the work and suffering you have to endure to get "there."

Each time you are faced with the opportunity to create a change, you automatically evaluate the price of the change. If the price seems too high, you may not be willing to pay the price. You may then decide not to change and thus remain in inertia and momentum.

For instance, imagine that you want to go back to school to get a college degree. The pain of not having earned a degree is great. You have observed less qualified people with college degrees getting promoted over you. You also know that you would derive a lot of pleasure by obtaining your degree. You would earn more money, probably get a promotion, and also have the prestige of earning a college degree.

Unfortunately, the price is high. You might have to spend years of hard work and thousands of hard-earned dollars to acquire that degree. Ultimately, you might decide that the price is too high to pay, thereby letting the opportunity go.

Changing Your Point of View

Fortunately, the pain, pleasure, and price of change are not fixed quantities. Instead, they are subjective qualities that can be mentally altered. Remember that everything has its good side and its bad side. The pleasure you will receive "there," the pain you endure "here," and the price you will have to pay are really the story of the half-full/half-empty glass. The pain you remove or the pleasure you attain is the half-full glass. The price you have to pay is the half-empty glass. What you ultimately do depends upon the half of the glass on which you concentrate your energies.

Vince Lombardi knew the secret of focusing on the half-full glass. He motivated his players by helping them to focus on the positive side of each situation. In one of my favorite quotations, he once said,

"In each player's heart is a dream and a hurt. When I concentrate on the injury, a synergy takes place and the hurt grows. Pretty soon, the player can think of nothing else, and drops out. When I think and speak of positive dreams a different synergy takes place. It blazes! It sparkles! Soon the hurt is forgotten. The life-force of the player is called up. Therefore, I only talk of dreams."

You too can become motivated when you concentrate on the positive, on the benefits of creating a change. But if you allow your focus to shift to the price, to all the work that you have to do and the possible pain you may have to endure, you may lose your motivation.

I remember how my enthusiasm was altered when my point of view was changed. For a Japanese kid in high school, I was pretty large. I remember walking across the campus when the football coach spotted me. He stopped me, looked me over and said, "I want to see you in my office today, after school."

I agreed and went to his office after school. He asked me to sit down and began to almost preach about football.

"Son," he said, "let me tell you about football. In this school, football is really big. Football players are looked up to here, and I think you have got what it takes. If you're willing to work hard and practice hard, I think you can be a great player. If you really work hard, you can maybe get a college scholarship. And who knows, if you really practice and apply yourself, maybe even get to play pro ball. That's where the big money is, you know. And one more thing son. Football players are really respected on this campus. If you're a star, the girls will be all over you."

Was I motivated? You bet!

He then handed me a slip of paper and said, "Okay. Take this release form home and have your parents sign it."

That evening I handed my father the form and announced that I wanted to play football. I explained to my father why I really had to play.

My father read the form, asked me to sit down, and began to talk.

"Son," he began, "let me tell you about football. Football is about pain. Football is about a lot of pain and injuries. And son, some of the injuries may be permanent. You might end up being crippled or paralyzed for the rest of your life. And son, you might even be good enough to qualify for a scholarship. But pro ball, only one in ten thousand makes it. You won't make it son. I would give it up if I were you."

Was I motivated to play football now? Not on your life! Why not? Because my father had changed my point of view. He had made me aware of the half-empty glass, the downside of playing football. He had helped me to realize that the price of playing football was really high.

The coach, who spoke to me first, had me excited about playing football. He had talked about the benefits of playing the game. He had made me look at the half-full glass. I was ready to do whatever it took to be a football "star."

Unfortunately for the coach, my father had spoken to me last. By focusing my impressionable mind on the high price of playing football, he had dumped ice water on my enthusiasm. He did not have to say anything else. I simply walked over to him, took the release form, and tore it up. I never did play football.

Focusing on the Positive

Motivation is your ability to focus mentally on the benefits and minimize the price you have to pay. As long as you remain focused on what you want to accomplish and the pain you can remove, the price you have to pay appears small.

This is usually easy to do when you first embark on your journey. But as the actual work makes you realize how high a price you have to pay, it can become increasingly more difficult to maintain your focus on the benefits. Unfortunately, most people are unable to maintain that positive focus. Instead, faced with the daily grind of hard work, they quit. In most cases, they quit on the eve of success. Success comes to those who are willing to follow through despite the trials, in order to attain the benefits they truly desire. To help you to focus on the positive, ask yourself the following questions:

- What pain will I remove by making this change?
- What reward (pleasure) will I receive by making this change?
- How can I minimize the price of making this change?

  Who will support my efforts?

  What can I do to make it faster, easier, or less painful?
- Is what I am about to undertake simply a personal test to see whether I can do it?

Answering the questions above lets you identify your motivators. You can be motivated by the amount of pain to be removed and the pleasure to be received. Minimizing the price of change can increase your chances of successfully creating the change.

Something Significant

Another method to increase your motivation is to participate in something significant. When you are a part of a significant activity, you are automatically motivated and tend to remain motivated. For instance, in times of disaster, no one has to motivate the rescuers to keep on working. It gives them personal pleasure to feel that they are contributing to something important. In fact, they are so motivated that the police and medical personnel often have to order them to stop and rest, take a few minutes to eat, or get some sleep.

Do you remember the national news story some years ago about a young girl who was trapped in a tiny mining shaft? The only way to rescue her was to drill a parallel shaft and then tunnel over to her. Over a period of several days, hundreds of people expended a tremendous amount of effort to save her life. Miners and construction workers worked around the clock. No one had to motivate them. If anything, doctors had to stop some of them when they were approaching the point of total exhaustion. From around the country, people and organizations were lending more than their moral support. They were willing to provide money, equipment, and manpower in the effort to save the little girl. With such a motivated team, she was rescued successfully.

People are always motivated to do their best when they are helping others in a significant way. *To become a part of something significant may require only a shift in your point of view.* If a photographer sees himself or herself on just another moneymaking gig, he or she is not motivated to do anything special. The job becomes just a lot of work. But suppose that same photographer could simply shift his or her point of view and see the job as an effort to preserve important memories for someone. As the photographer focuses on the benefits, he or she may be motivated enough to go the extra mile.

A cook is a cook if he or she simply works to prepare food for people. A cook becomes a true chef when preparing food from the heart that nourishes souls with beautiful presentations and unique flavors. A teacher struggles at a job to teach students a skill. A teacher becomes an educator when he or she is shaping a community and helping students to succeed in life. When you shift your focus to something more than routine work, you become motivated to do your best.

As a speaker, I am always motivated when I give a presentation. You see, I never go to a presentation just to give a presentation. I know I am usually there to help at least one person improve his or her life. Unfortunately, I do not know who this person is. It may be a quiet person in the back of the room or an enthusiastic person in the front row. But because I have no idea which person I may be touching, I always give my best presentation.

The people whom I have helped are also helping me. It touches me to think that something I have shared has the power to help another person through his or her difficulties. Even when I have to work long hours or travel to far-off places, I always remain motivated.

As I am writing this, one person comes to mind. I had completed my speech and was packing up my equipment. Just as I was getting ready to leave, a man approached me. He shook my hand and said, "I heard you three years ago and I spoke to you afterwards. Do you remember me?"

I looked closely at him and searched for my memory for some glimmer of recognition. But with the thousands of people I meet, it can be difficult to remember one specific person. I wanted to say yes, but answered an honest, "No."

"Well . . . you spoke to my group and I thanked you afterward. You know, you made a profound difference in my life. You picked me up when I was down. You gave me the words I needed to hear."

These are the rewards of my profession. However, the thanks are not as important to me as the simple fact that I have helped people to make their lives better. Just this past week, I received a call from New Zealand and one from Canada from people whom I have touched in some way. They are now taking my message and helping other people. Helping people, doing something significant to help others improve their lives, keeps me motivated. What is it that keeps you ticking?

Something Personal

You are also motivated to do things that have a personal impact on your life. A scientist may not have much desire to participate in research to find a cure for a rare disease that will do very little for his or her career. But if someone in the scientist's family suddenly comes down with that rare disease, the motivation will automatically be there.

I always remember the story of Father Flanagan and the boy who arrived carrying his brother on his back. When Father Flanagan asked the boy if the child he carried was heavy, the boy simply replied, "He's not heavy, Father, he's my brother."

The boy did not focus on the price, which was the work involved in carrying his brother. He was focusing only on the benefits. He was motivated and his load was light. If you are personally involved with the outcome, you will always be more motivated.

Motivation is a game that is played inside your head. It is totally determined by how you process the situations with which you are faced. As soon as you shift your focus from the price of change to the benefits you will receive (less pain and greater pleasure), your enthusiasm increases.

When you have great skills and demonstrate self-motivation, you are viewed as a hard worker. In the Information Age, hard work is not enough. In Step 2, you will learn how to increase your knowledge and communication skills to become even better.

Step 2
Work Smart
(ability)

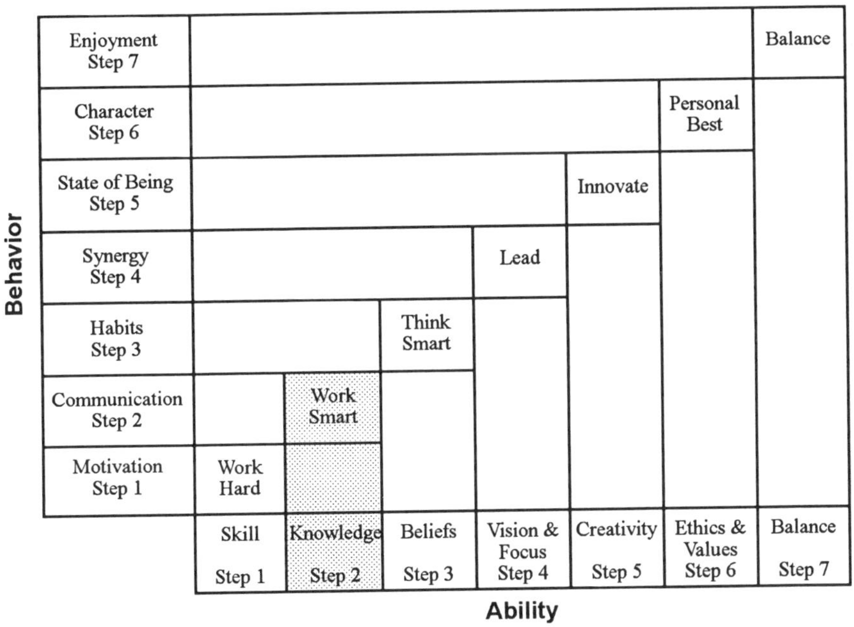

Chapter 5

Step 2: Work Smart (ability)

Knowledge: Constant Learning

Education will not simply be a prelude to a career, but a lifelong endeavor.
— Maud Barkley

Moving on to Step 2 prepares you to move to another level. Career advancement becomes possible when you move beyond perfecting skills and begin acquiring knowledge. Knowledge gives you the ability to understand "why" things happen. The more knowledge you acquire on a wider range of related topics, the greater your professional potential becomes.

As I mentioned earlier, people with skills know "how" things are done and always have a job. *The people who know "why" things happen are the ones who lead them.* They are the ones who supervise those who possess only skills.

Commit to Educating Yourself

Carl Sagan has wisely pointed out that in stable times, stable species thrive while rapidly mutating species became extinct. However, in rapidly changing times, the stable species become extinct while the evolving species thrive.

You and I are in the midst of rapidly changing times. You are now living at the beginning of the Information Age. To evolve and thrive in this age, you must assume responsibility for your own education. You cannot leave this important task to the whims of others. You must commit yourself to the process of continuous lifelong education.

You can begin by mastering the art of learning: simplifying the process of extracting useful information, and then converting it into knowledge. In the Information Age, knowledge and the ability to apply that knowledge are the sources of true power.

Information and More Information

The primary product of the Information Age is information. You are experiencing a torrential downpour of information today, more than you can even imagine. It is currently estimated that the total amount of information gathered from the beginning of recorded time will double every five years. You are being flooded with information from computer networks, newspapers, television reports, magazines, books, special reports, faxes, and the mail.

Even this flood of information would not be so much of a problem if everything you received were accurate and useful. Unfortunately, the information you receive is often inaccurate, incorrect, or partially correct. It may carry a biased viewpoint. Occasionally, you even receive information that is completely fraudulent.

On top of this, most of the deluge of information that floods your senses is of no interest to you. It has no real application in your life. There is a simple test to see whether any piece of information is important. Consider the data and then simply ask yourself, "So what?" If there is no significant answer to the question, the information is of little use to you and you should throw it out immediately.

From all the information you gather, you gain knowledge. Knowledge consists of a few basic principles you have extracted from the information. As you struggle to pick out knowledge from the unending information flood, you may begin to feel overwhelmed.

Remember when Alice, from *Alice in Wonderland*, was running as fast as she could and was not getting anywhere? The Queen told Alice that she had to run as fast as she could just to stay in the same place. If she wanted to get anywhere else, she had to run even faster than that.

This seems to be what is happening to everyone. How do you keep up? There is no simple solution. But there are a few methods that can simplify your acquisition of knowledge.

Hire Expertise

Determine where you are most productive, and hire the rest out. As an electronic engineer with a lot of background in computers and communications, I always prided myself in my ability to keep up with the computer industry. I understood the basics of the computer hardware and also knew how to do software programming. But as computer technological advancements accelerated, it became increasingly more difficult for me to keep up with the changes. Finally, in 1993, I concluded that I was spending too much of my precious time working on my computers. I would struggle for hours trying to get a new program or system to work.

One day, while struggling with an especially difficult computer problem, I finally realized that working on computers was not my main business. As a professional speaker, facilitator, and consultant, I earned a living through marketing and speaking. The computer was only a tool to help me become more effective.

Since that day, I have not worked on any of my computer systems. I have my computer "guru" who takes care of my computer problems. Shortly after making that decision, I was at a party with some friends. I noticed that one of the guests arrived nearly two hours late. When I asked why, he told me he had just bought a hard disk drive at a discount store. He and another friend had spent over ten hours trying to get the hard disk to work. After all that time, the system still did not work.

By coincidence, I had a similar hard disk installed in one of my computers a week earlier. To install my hard disk, I called my "computer guru" and had him install it. He then tested it on my system network and made sure it worked perfectly. The final bill was about forty dollars more than it would have been if I had purchased it at the discount store. My time and freedom from stress were certainly worth much more than that.

As a solution to my friend's problem, I offered to give him the phone number of my computer guru. The two of them had lost a whole day and ended up spending even more money by not hiring expertise.

Oh, I still do simple application programming to accomplish the results I want. But I leave all my equipment upgrades, new systems, and networking problems to my computer guru. If a computer problem comes up, I call him and he fixes it. Each time I see him or one of his people at work on my computers, I realize how much time and energy he is saving me.

In almost every field, there are experts who can solve almost every problem. I now have a publishing guru to help me with publishing. I have an audiotape guru and a videotape guru. Time has become today's most precious commodity. It is more economical and practical to hire an expert than to save a little money and waste a lot of time trying to make today's complex systems work by yourself!

Continuous Education

You need to take the time to increase your knowledge base. If you are doing the same thing today that you did a year ago, you are already becoming obsolete. To keep up with the latest changes in your field, you must update your knowledge regularly.

At one time, education was usually obtained through college and university programs. In today's fast-paced lifestyle, however, few can afford the luxury of going back to school. The new sources of education must be more flexible, providing you with a broad education on a just-in-time basis.

One way to stay current is to join a professional association of people who are in the same field. Professional associations often make professional subject matter experts available to you. They also offer you the advantage of networking with others in your field.

Surprisingly, it is often your competitors who know more about your business than anyone else. It is they who can offer key insights on how to increase your performance. In a rapidly changing environment, your ability to succeed is often determined by the number of people you know who are willing to advise and support you. Of course, you are expected to reciprocate and share your knowledge with them.

If you want additional learning resources, there are all types of educational sources available. Beyond traditional schools and colleges, you can educate yourself through books, audio- and videotapes, the Internet, seminars, magazines, newspapers, newsletters, and CD-ROM (Compact Disk Read-Only Memory). However, staying up-to-date can quickly become overwhelming.

To make yourself more effective, you must stop reading everything that catches your fancy or crosses your mailbox. You have to sort through and separate useful information from the dross. A computer on-line service will allow you to accomplish this efficiently with magazines and newspapers. It can identify specific topics that you can read to obtain just the information you desire.

You can also subscribe to a book digest service, which simplifies the books you want to read. And you can also enlist the use of books on audiotape and listen to them while you drive.

Beyond Continuous Learning

With the sheer volume of information being given to you, you have to go beyond continuous learning and develop a method of systematically gaining new information. Then you must store this information efficiently and be able to find it fast.

The following is an effective tactic for gaining as much useful information as possible in the shortest possible time:

1. Get the gist of the material.
2. Commit to continuous updating.
3. Decide what to eliminate.
4. Review new information regularly.
5. Make use of nonproductive time.

Get The Gist of the Material

Whether you are reading a book or listening to a speaker or an instructional audiotape, you have to extract information efficiently. If you take a lot of notes, you may find the following method useful.

At one time, I was a compulsive note-taking junkie. I would take pages of notes from a single seminar. This all changed the day I attended a seminar given by a friend. As usual, I sat close to the front. After the first hour of a two-hour seminar, we had a short break. My friend began speaking to the young man sitting next to me.

"I noticed that compared to everyone else, you aren't writing down very much in your notepad."

The young man nodded and said, "I took down everything you said."

I looked at his notepad. He had two lines of a strange scribble written on it. I, on the other hand, had filled mine with six pages of notes.

"You didn't write very much," commented my friend.

"You didn't say very much," countered the young man.

The young man began to explain that he had learned a new language that reduced information to its pure, basic form. What my friend had said in fifteen minutes could be reduced to a short scribble. When the seminar was over, the young man had written a total of five lines. Apparently my friend had really gone all out and covered a lot more content during the second hour than he had during the first!

That night, as I thought about the incident, I realized that we communicate with a lot of "fillers." I looked at my bookshelves filled with books and notebooks that time and changes had made useless. I got up and immediately began throwing out all my old notes and gave away about half of my books.

I was also intrigued with the idea of a new and extremely efficient language to communicate basic ideas. But the idea of learning a completely new language did not excite me. Instead, I devised a scheme to simplify my own learning process. I use it for the books I read, seminars and speeches I attend, and audio tapes I listen to. The rules I follow are the following:

1. Extract the gist of any new information.
2. Do not record any information you already know or use.
3. Ask, "Is this information useful?" If not, place it within parentheses.
4. Ask, "Do I agree with this information?" If not, place it within parentheses.
5. Ask, "Can I use this information now?" If yes, make a note on how to use it.
6. Enter this information into your computer; print it out. Review it regularly.

As a professional speaker, the only exception I make to my system is with quotations. I find quotations very useful and I write them out completely. I put the notes in a folder and review them every few months.

By itself, information is not useful. To become useful, information has to be transformed into knowledge. You must cull it until you extract its useful essence.

Commit to Continuous Updating

To achieve maximum effectiveness and peak performance levels, you must never let the process of learning stop. To remain ahead, you must continuously upgrade your knowledge. To help you achieve this, I have a few more suggestions:

1. Read at least one nonfiction book a month.

   Note only what is useful or novel.

   Store useful information in a database.

2. Listen to at least one audiotape program every other month.
3. Attend at least one business seminar a year.
4. Join and participate in a professional association.

   Be an active member and participate.

5. Network with at least one new person a month.

   Pick someone with interests different from yours.

6. Once a year, learn something completely new.

   Learn something counter to your present beliefs.

   See what new ideas or approaches it triggers.

7. Consider your life from the opposite point of view.

   Take a moment to see things differently.

   Try to understand other people's viewpoints.

8. Stop believing that you are an expert in your field.

   Experts are limited by their present paradigms.

   Stop defending your "expert" positions.

   Be open-minded so that you will recognize upcoming trends.

9. Know where to get information when you need it.

   Become familiar with various sources of information.

Become familiar with sources that can give you the information that you need quickly. The library, the Internet, and experts in various fields are all great assets you need to know how to tap. The greater your resources, the greater your ability to excel.

Decide What to Eliminate

Another way of increasing your knowledge base is knowing what information to eliminate, and when to do it. In fact, gathering new information is the least of your problems. Sources of information are everywhere. The real problem is getting rid of all the old, useless information stored in your mind and in your file cabinets.

The average half-life of information is about five years. In other words, half of all the information in the world will become obsolete in five years. It becomes obvious that if you are going to excel, you will have to be willing and able to discard half of what you know every five years.

Unfortunately, there is no efficient way to release old information. You can only maintain an open mind to all new ideas, even those that go counter to present wisdom. Otherwise, the glut of now "useless" information will prevent you from acquiring and applying new ideas.

Review New Information Regularly

A lot of the information offered to you is not *presently* useful. This does not mean that you should discard it immediately. When a novel idea is proposed by someone, make a note of it. Even if you have no use for that information right now, you should store it for possible future use.

You can then review your collection of ideas regularly. What appears to be useless today may not be so tomorrow. A little time sometimes unveils the power of an idea.

When I review my notes, I ask myself the following questions:

1. Have I implemented this information?
2. Is the information still of interest?
3. Do I now agree with what I originally thought was false?
4. Can I use this information now? If so, how?

If the new idea does not prove to be useful in a couple of years, it is probably safe to purge your notes. There is always a chance that it will become useful someday, but if its usefulness did not become apparent within a couple of years, the chances are remote.

Make Use of Nonproductive Time

Here are some ways in which I use my nonproductive time to keep myself upgraded: When commuting, I sometimes listen to an audiotape program. I often turn my automobile into a concert hall and use it to remove any stress I have acquired during the day.

You can also create your own audiotape. Collect the best ideas and thoughts you have found over the last year and record them on a tape. Then, as you drive to and from work, you can listen to these ideas and try to discover ways of implementing them to further your career or your personal life.

You can benefit from the time you spend waiting for someone by reading a book. You can also use that time to meditate or listen to music to relieve stress. It is not difficult to make better use of nonproductive time.

Having additional knowledge is still not enough in order to "work smart." In the next chapter, you will learn to communicate your knowledge in order to become more effective.

Step 2
Work Smart
(behavior)

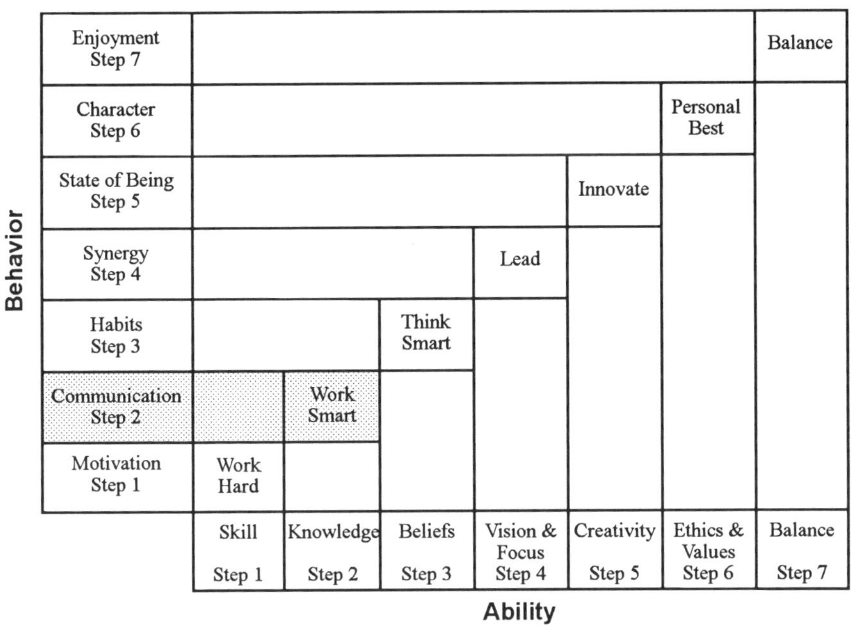

Chapter 6
Step 2: Work Smart (behavior)
Communication: Increasing Effectiveness

You can have brilliant ideas, but if you can't get them across, your ideas won't get you anywhere. — Lee Iacocca

Great knowledge without the ability to communicate that knowledge is of little use. You must be able to communicate your ideas to co-workers and management to achieve the right results. Your ability to communicate information accurately, transmitting exactly what you intend and receiving what the other person intended, gives you tremendous power. You must learn how your every gesture, facial expression, and voice inflection broadcasts all kinds of information that everyone picks up subliminally.

An example of poor communication happened when my wife and I recently decided to purchase a new car. We had narrowed our choices down to two models and decided it was time to bite the bullet and deal with a salesperson. Walking into the first dealership, we were immediately met by a smiling salesman. He walked around the lot with us, showing us what he had in stock. We took a short test drive and liked the way the car drove. We ended up in his cubicle to discuss the price. The price he quoted was very good, but we said that we had to "sleep" on our decision. As we were driving out of the lot, I asked my wife what she thought.

She looked at me and said, "Sleeeeze! The guy is so sleazy. I wouldn't buy a car from him if he were the only salesperson in town!"

"My thoughts exactly!" I agreed.

The man did and said everything right. He was dressed professionally. He accompanied us around the lot and showed us whatever we wanted to look at. He told us everything we wanted to know and gave us a decent price. But from the time we met him, he was saying to us, "I am not the type of person you can trust."

Now you may be thinking, "Right, Gary, but maybe that's because you and your wife are so sensitive."

Well, I told this story at a number of seminars that I held in Tucson, where I live. Almost invariably, someone asked which dealership. When I mentioned the name, a few people immediately pinpointed the exact salesperson I was talking about. In one particular seminar of about thirty-five people, seven people knew the salesperson.

It is not because my wife and I are sensitive. Everyone is capable of picking up another person's subliminal messages. In the same manner, other people are picking up *your* subliminal messages. My parents are experts at it. My in-laws do it with astounding accuracy. A few of my close friends are uncanny. These are not special people. People today are just so much more sophisticated and sensitive. They are often able to discern the real person beneath the act being presented to the world.

Several years ago, I had another incident that really made me aware of how much we communicate on a subliminal level. A person came to me for a private consultation. When he arrived, I asked him to have a seat. I then discovered I had left my notepad in the other room and excused myself to get it.

When I walked back in, the man asked, "Gary, have you done a lot of martial arts?" He paused for a couple of seconds, then continued, "I mean, have you had a lot of martial arts training, like aikido?"

I looked at him in total amazement. Yes, I had had a lot of martial arts training. For about twenty-two years, I had practiced that very martial art of aikido. I could only answer, "Yes, why do you ask?"

"Oh," he answered, "I just knew you did."

"Are you a psychic?"

"Oh no," he laughed. "You see, I'm a police officer. In my profession, I need to be aware of people. Whenever I see anyone, I automatically size them up . . . you know, try to figure out where they're coming from. Anyway, I could tell by the way you walked and moved that you had a lot of martial arts training."

That afternoon, after the man had left, I began to observe myself as I walked in front of my bathroom mirror. Later I stared at my reflection in store windows. I was really studying how I walked. I was trying to see what that police officer had seen. For a few days, I became so self-conscious that walking became uncomfortable.

The police officer may have seemed a bit exceptional, but he was not the exception. People are constantly reading body language in singles bars or on the beach. Criminals do it to size up a potential victim. My friend and fellow speaker, Mike Hayashi, teaches people how to keep themselves from becoming victims. He shows them how to change their body language so that they are not nonverbally screaming to potential criminals, "Hey, here I am! I am ready to be victimized! Come and get me!"

To communicate more accurately, you have to understand exactly what information you are transmitting and how you can improve on what you are subliminally saying to others.

The Human Transmitter

Whenever you say something to someone, you are transmitting information on three levels. You communicate through the words you speak, the inflection and tone of your voice, and your body language.

Words And More Words

Of course the words you choose are important in communication, especially written communication. In letters, memos, and notes you write, you do not have the luxury of using your voice inflection and body language. Every bit of information is carried in the words you choose.

In our modern Communication Age, the ability to communicate through writing is again becoming critical. The widespread use of faxes, computers, and the Internet requires a good command of writing skills. To ensure that the right message is being conveyed, you must check every single word carefully.

In business you must also learn to communicate information quickly. People do not have time for a long explanation that comes to a conclusion at the very end. Instead, start with the bottom line and then follow that with your explanation. This way, your correspondence is more likely to be read and taken seriously.

The Music of Speaking

Unlike written communication, speech carries a tremendous subliminal message to the listener. It is transmitted through your voice inflection and tone, and through your body language.

Your voice inflection and tone convey a lot of information. More than communicating simple words, facts, and ideas, your voice tone also communicates your feelings. With the proper volume, inflection, and tone, you can let the listener know how you are feeling.

Unfortunately, no one ever taught me how to share my feelings by modulating my voice. I was always told that I should raise my voice tone at the end of a question. Other than that, I never really learned how to use my voice to communicate more effectively.

I did notice, however, that anyone who spoke in a monotone would quickly put the audience, including me, to sleep. While I was also guilty of speaking in a monotone, this trait never really mattered until I began to speak in front of an audience. Suddenly, the ability to use my voice more effectively became extremely important. My wife became my unsolicited voice coach. She kept telling me that I should stop speaking so softly and to vary my voice tones and inflection. If I wanted to succeed as a speaker, I knew I had to stop speaking in a monotone. Unfortunately, I had no idea where to begin.

Speaking with a range of tones just seemed totally out of character. After all, I had survived for most of my life speaking in a quiet monotone. This was a part of my upbringing. Japanese people are supposed to be calm and quiet. Engineers are supposed to be mental people, deep thinkers. Martial artists are supposed to be in control, not easily excited. All this attention on my speaking seemed so esoteric and frivolous. After all, it was my *message* the people needed to hear, right?

One day, while channel surfing, I stumbled on a public television program in which they were discussing how emotions are conveyed through music. They showed how the tone fluctuated when the music conveyed sorrow, happiness, excitement, anger, and so on. I was intrigued and I immediately knew that this was very important. This was the key I had been looking for! This would definitely help me to communicate my feelings. I also realized that it would help others to be more interesting, dynamic, and effective communicators. I quickly copied down the diagrams shown below:

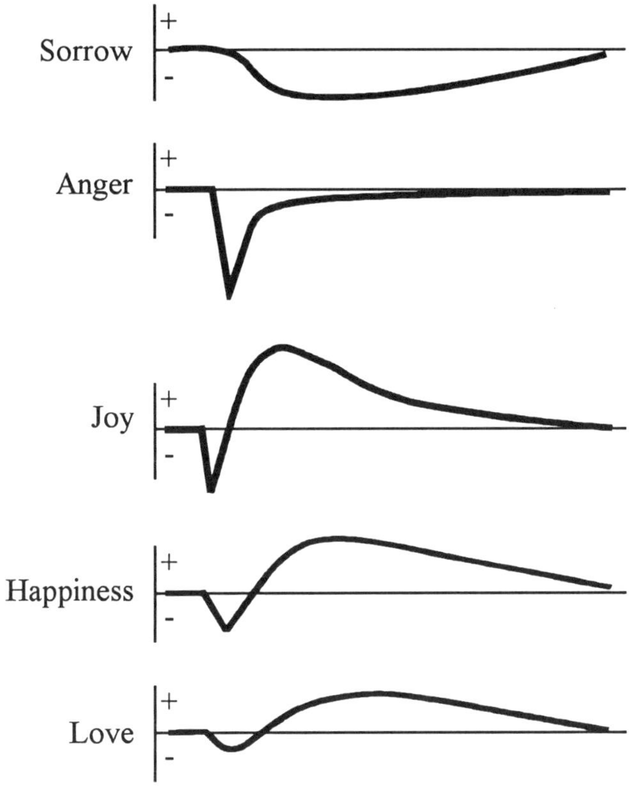

Figure 6-1: Tonal Changes Associated with Feelings

To use these diagrams to communicate feelings, practice using the tones shown. The best way to isolate and concentrate only on your voice tone is to practice communicating without using any words. Try to communicate by humming. When the line goes up, raise the pitch of your voice. When it goes down, lower your pitch. When the line goes up sharply, raise your pitch quickly. Conversely, when it drops sharply, lower your pitch quickly.

Thus, the music of the emotion of sorrow is a dropping tone, which slowly rises to its original tone. Happiness, on the other hand, is the opposite. It rises quickly and then drops off slowly.

When you have control over your vocal tone, you can practice it with words. Pick a simple statement, such as, "Hi, I'm feeling great today." Notice that the tone for each word, or group of words, can be altered to change the emotion. The tonal fluctuations that you place on each word tell the listener exactly how you feel about that word.

Now practice saying the same thing with different emotions. First say it as if you were truly happy. Then say it as if you were angry. When you can do this at will, you will have perfected your ability to control the "music" of your speaking — and the emotions it conveys.

Your ability to change the tone of your voice is especially important when you communicate over the telephone. Unless your voice tones agree with the words you are saying, people will tend to believe the subliminal message that comes from the voice tone instead of the words you are saying.

For this reason, a basic class in telephone skills often requires that you look at yourself in a mirror and smile as you speak over the phone. You do this because the person on the other end is actually able to hear the subtle difference between someone who is smiling and someone who is not. When you have mastered the art of communicating emotions by controlling your voice tone, your effectiveness as a communicator will improve significantly.

Body Talk

Your body language also carries a lot of your subliminal message. Every gesture you make conveys a message. Therefore, the way you stand, sit, dress, place your hands, and even cross your legs are all broadcasting information to your listener. If your body language is not in agreement with what you are saying, your listener will not believe your message.

In fact there are rules that cover every aspect of body talk, and many books cover this subject in detail. They provide so many rules to remember and master. And you are expected to perform perfectly, to the most discerning and aware audience on the planet — your prospective customers, your family members, and your co-workers. How many of them can you fool? Perhaps this is not the right question to ask. The right question may be, "Can you really fool anyone?"

They Can See Your Thoughts

I once heard a wonderful speaker offer suggestions on delivering effective, dynamic presentations to large audiences. She said that when the audience is larger than about two hundred people, the meeting planner usually has the speaker's image projected onto a large screen. Except for those in the very front row, everyone looks at your enlarged image on the screen. When your face is being projected so that it is fifteen feet high and twenty feet wide, the audience can see everything. Everything! She said, "Your audience can even see what you are thinking."

That statement had a great impact on me. She also mentioned that because movie actors and actresses have their faces projected onto huge screens, they, too, appear so much larger than life, and the audience can see what they are thinking.

This is one of the major reasons that actors and actresses are paid so much money. The best of them are able to take on a different persona. At some point, they stop acting and become the people they are playing. This is why they appear so natural. This is the reason you and I are able to believe that they really are the people they are portraying. We believe that we are peering into their personal lives.

Unfortunately, most people are not great actors or actresses. They have not been formally trained and have not spent years studying and perfecting the art. For this reason, you and I can subliminally pick up what these people are really feeling and thinking. We can distinguish the "sleaze" from someone who is earnest.

If you can pick up this information from other people, they are probably receiving the same information from you. Years of acting classes might solve this problem. Alternatively, you can do something completely different. *To communicate an authentic message, you have to become authentic.*

Authentic Communication

Authenticity may sound like a radical idea! In other words, you must really *feel* what you are trying to communicate. Even when you do not feel like caring about the other person, you have to do it.

When you care about the other person, your communication will change. The great motivational speaker Cavett Robert has said, "People don't care what you are selling until they know you care about them." You can extend what Cavett said about selling to include every other activity. *People do not care about you until they know you care about them.*

Is it possible for you to really care about a stranger? One simple method is to place yourself in their shoes. Ask yourself, "If I were in that person's place, what would I want to experience from me?"

If service people could authentically care about another person, a lot of customer service problems would disappear. They would speak kindly to every customer, making sure to do their best to solve all of the customer's concerns and problems with their products or services. They would do the job right, on time, and at a fair price, or else they would effectively communicate why the customer's expectation could not be met.

If more people cared about their fellow workers, the workplace would change dramatically. People would begin supporting each other instead of trying to raise themselves up by knocking others down. The "lone rangers" of the organization would disappear and teamwork would become commonplace. The workplace culture would never be the same.

If people cared, they would harbor positive thoughts about other people. They would not be thinking, "What a fat guy," or "That woman must have had a couple of face lifts." If their thinking were filled with caring, the message they projected would be positive. Imagine an organization filled with people who authentically care about their customers and communicate that feeling! This is the type of organization people can and will trust. When customers and clients trust an organization, they repeatedly do business with that organization.

Caring will also benefit you personally. At some point in your life, you will be recognized as being someone special because you care.

A Time to Listen

Listening is the other half of communication. The next time you have the opportunity, listen to a television message from the president of the United States. After the speech, a couple of people will come on to make some comments about the president's speech. These people are "spin doctors," whose job is to clarify, attack, or "twist" the president's message.

The spokesperson for the opposite party will say, "The president is *really* saying . . . This is terrible for the country!"

Right after that person, a presidential supporter may then come out and say, "No, that is not what the president meant. What he *really* said was . . . This is really good for the country!"

Spin doctors take a speech and try to alter what was said. They represent themselves as experts who try to put the right spin or twist on what the speaker has just said. If the message supported their ideas, they will praise the speaker and the speech. If the message did not support their ideas, they will try to ridicule or destroy both the message and the messenger.

What You Heard Was Not What Was Said

In your mind, you have your own personal spin doctor. Your spin doctor constantly alters the messages you receive. *It alters every message instantly, without your conscious knowledge.*

Imagine that someone is speaking to you and giving you a message. As soon as you begin hearing the message, your internal spin doctor begins to alter the information in one of the following ways:

1. If you like either the person or the message, you will automatically support both the message and the messenger.
2. If you hate either the person or the message, you will put down, criticize, or ridicule the message and the messenger.
3. A strong belief regarding one part of the message may authenticate the rest of the message and the messenger.
4. A strong bias against one part of the message may diminish the rest of the message and maybe the messenger.
5. If the messenger is ineffective in communicating the message, the message may be lost. You may ridicule the messenger and downplay the message. The messenger may be ineffective because of a heavy accent, the use of technical jargon, or the inclusion of industry-specific acronyms.

6. If you are not interested in the message topic, you may totally disregard the message.
7. If what the messenger says conflicts with his or her voice tone and body language, you may not believe the words.

Your personal spin doctor colors everything you experience. In the end, what you thought you heard may not be what the speaker meant.

What Others Hear

When you write or speak to another person, you must deal with that person's own personal spin doctor. Every person you speak to has his or her own agenda, personal desires, prejudices, and fears. Each of these desires, prejudices, and fears can be represented as a sensitivity button sticking out of the person's body. One sensitivity button may say, "I believe in UFOs, and you'd better not talk down to or make fun of people who believe as I do!" Another button may declare, "You'd better not treat women differently from men. In fact, you should treat women better than men." And still another may announce, "I'm a teacher and you'd better not criticize us or the educational system."

Each person may have hundreds of these sensitivity buttons sticking out. Anytime you say anything "wrong," especially if it is new, different, profound, or on the cutting edge, you will invariably push the other person's buttons. From that moment, he or she will have a prejudice against you or what you are saying.

If you want to avoid offending others, you must be sure that you say the politically/ethnically/racially/sexually "correct" thing. Being "correct" means not saying anything new, controversial, different, or profound. In other words, you may talk about the weather but not criticize it.

Compensating for Your Buttons

There is a simple rule I always use when communicating with others. I try to speak or write to the best of my ability. Then, if what I say or write bothers the other person, I feel that it is not my problem, but theirs. Conversely, if what they say bothers me, I view it as my problem.

To help you remember this rule, say the following out loud:

"I always do my best. If it bothers them, it's their problem. If it bothers me, it's my problem."

Now if something about another person bothers you, you do not have to change that person. You can change yourself. You can either remove the sensitivity button (which may be difficult to do), or remove yourself from the company of the offending person. In either case, the choice is yours. You have the power to create a change.

At the same time, remember that communication is the process of learning what the other person has to offer. If you find the other person pushing one of your hair-trigger sensitivity buttons, be aware of it and try to maintain an open mind. See whether there is anything you can learn from the other person. I am always intrigued to see what I can learn.

The Art of Listening

To really understand what another person is trying to say, you have to listen carefully. Because of lack of interest, boredom, or physical or mental exhaustion, you may miss the real message the other person is trying to communicate. You may also be distracted by an external event or by thinking about what you are going to say next.

However, even your full attention may not be enough to comprehend the total message. You must also listen and hear what the other person cannot communicate verbally.

What Cannot Be Communicated

Many times another person cannot communicate his or her real message. More than listening skills, it often takes luck to determine what the messenger is not saying. The following are some common reasons that the person does not convey the real message:

1. The other person may feel that the message is not appropriate for you and therefore censures a portion of it.
2. The other person avoids mentioning something because, knowing your prejudices and fears, he or she does not want to hurt, anger, or embarrass you.

3. The other person avoids saying something that will embarrass him or her.
4. The other person assumes that you know more than you really do.

Sometimes the other person may withhold information from you. There is no formula or technique that can supply you with what was not said. Instead, when you listen carefully, you can develop an almost intuitive sense of any underlying messages. You can learn to fill in the missing gaps instinctively.

Feedback

Listening is an art that is perfected with practice. Everything you hear and read is being altered by your internal spin doctor. You can minimize the spin doctor's effect by receiving feedback from the other person. When you hear something you find questionable, you can ask,

"Correct me if I'm wrong, but did you say . . ." or,

"Let me be sure I got this correct. Did you mean . . ."

Feedback is a face-saving way to make sure that you perceived the information correctly. When you speak, you can give automatic feedback by saying,

"So the bottom line of what I'm are saying is . . ." or,

"What this really boils down to is . . ."

The more feedback you give and receive, the greater the possibility that the information will be accurate. The more you practice giving feedback, the easier it becomes to experience meaningful communication.

The Next Level of Communication

Your words, tone of voice, and body language do not constitute the limits of communication. There is another significant form of communication, based on the feelings or sense we get from another person. This will be covered in detail in the chapter on state of being.

Step 3
Think Smart
(ability)

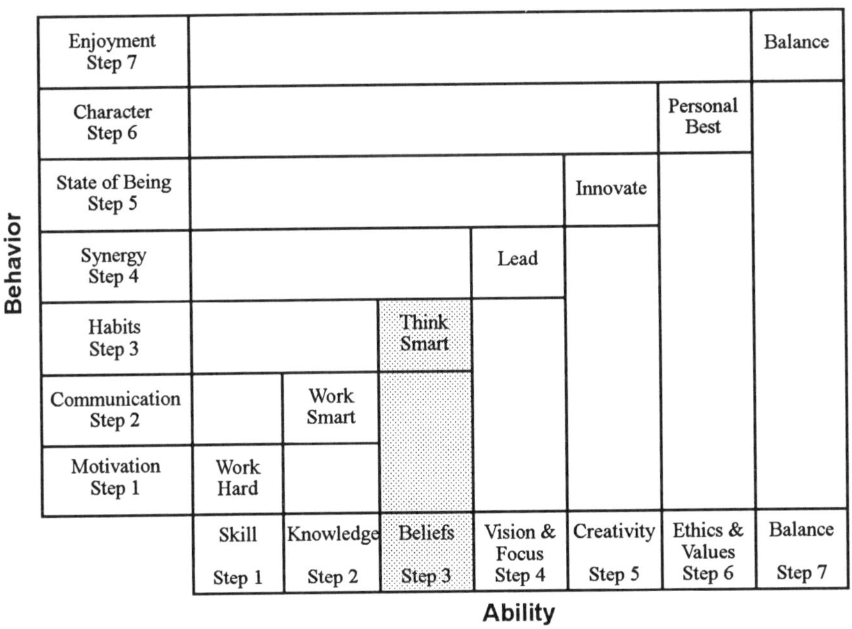

Chapter 7

Step 3: Think Smart (ability)

Beliefs: Unleashing Mental Power

Progress is impossible without change,
and those who cannot change their
minds cannot change anything.
— George Bernard Shaw

This chapter and the next concentrate on how to make significant and permanent changes in your life. Making a change is easy. Making a meaningful and permanent change is much more difficult. You must learn how to take your great ideas and transform your life.

Almost everyone has a tremendous amount of knowledge. For instance, we know what we should eat and how to exercise in order to be healthy. We know what to do to develop our job skills or improve our relationships. We know a lot of things we need to do, and we know exactly how to do them. But the bottom line problem for some people is simple: they just do not know how to get themselves to do these things consistently, for the rest of their lives.

The reason they fail is not because they are stupid. It is definitely not because they are lazy or lack willpower. The reason they fail to achieve lies deep within the contents of their subconscious mind.

Within our subconscious minds lies a powerful universe. This universe is below the level of our conscious minds. As such, it is not directly accessible to our thinking and rational minds. Living below our conscious awareness, our subconscious minds seem to have a life of their own. They are capable of rising up when we least expect it. They then control us, often taking us to places we may not wish to visit. This powerful subconscious force is our beliefs.

Brain Connections

As a child, you started life with a clean slate of beliefs. When a fact was given to you, your brain created a temporary connection and a thought was formed. When the thought ended, the connection was immediately dissolved. If the same thought was repeated over a period of time, the connection became permanent. This permanent connection became a belief.

The interrelationship between your beliefs and thoughts is shown below:

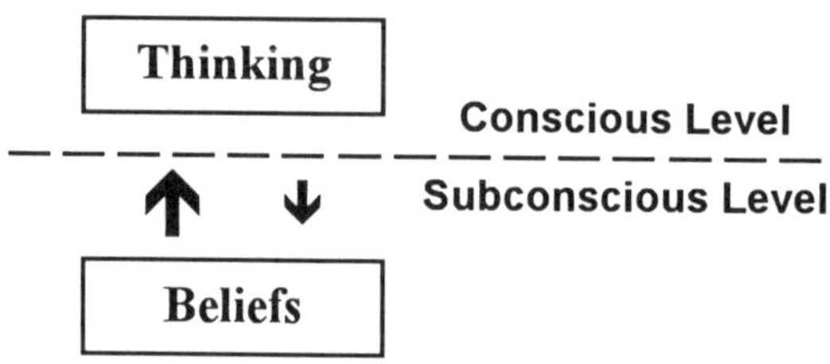

Figure 7-1: Interrelationship between Thoughts and Beliefs

As soon as a belief was created, it began to control your thoughts. Fortunately, your mind was very flexible when you were young. When you were given a new fact that contradicted your old belief, your mind simply created new connections and formed a new thought. Repetition solidified the new thought and it then became a belief. The brain connections that maintained your old belief simply disappeared from lack of use.

Momentum of Life

Somewhere around the age of eleven, your ability to easily change your beliefs diminished. Your beliefs began to take on a life of their own. They began to resist all new ideas and tried to maintain the status quo. This would not be a problem if all of your beliefs were accurate and useful.

Unfortunately, a major portion of your beliefs were formed when you were very young. The person who gave them to you may have been your parents, your teacher, a religious leader, or even your peers. Of course, the source of a belief could just as easily have been a magazine article, a comic book, or a television program.

Today when someone presents you with a new idea that goes against your present belief, you may find yourself automatically questioning or even rejecting the new idea. You may find yourself saying,

"I don't believe that," or "Only fools think that way."

Like everyone else, you have an almost natural tendency to reject or ridicule whatever goes counter to your existing beliefs. This tendency is the momentum of your mind. It wants you to maintain your old beliefs.

Beliefs and Reality

Your beliefs create your reality. Henry Ford said, "If you think you can or you think you can't, you're probably right."

I would like to modify that a little to read, "If you believe you can or you believe you can't, you're probably right."

Yes, this is a self-fulfilling system. If you can mentally accept something as possible, you can make it happen. (If it does not take place, you have not yet changed your existing belief that says "it will not happen.")

The classic example is the running of the mile in under four minutes. Since ancient Greece, this feat was believed to be impossible. All of the superathletes got close, but no one was able to do it. In spite of what the runners may have been saying to reporters and each other, they really believed that breaking the four-minute barrier was impossible.

Then one day, Roger Bannister showed up and ran the mile in under four minutes. When he did, everyone else's beliefs changed immediately. In the year following his record-breaking feat, more than a dozen runners were also able to break the barrier.

Right now you have beliefs about what you can and cannot do. What would happen if you were able to change those beliefs? What new activities could you take on? What new adventures would you undertake? What limits could you overcome if you believed it were now possible for you to break an "impossible" barrier?

Your Limiting Beliefs

At any moment, you have thousands of possible choices. Among the many career options you have, a few of them may be the following:

1. Quit your job and start your own business.
2. Transfer to another department.
3. Go back to school part-time.
4. Continue to do what you have always done.
5. Sell controlled substances.
6. Work harder and longer.
7. Take it easy and do as little as possible.

All of these are options, but your beliefs will limit them. If you believe in working within the legal constraints of the law, choice 5 is no longer a possibility. If you believe that you do not have enough business training to start your own business, choice 1 is out. If you believe that you do not have enough time to do anything else, choice 3 is eliminated. If you feel that the company is cutting back and eliminating problem people, choices 2, 4, and 7 are not viable. This only leaves choice 6.

In this manner, your life is largely controlled and limited by all of your beliefs. Your beliefs color what you perceive in the world around you. For instance, if you believe that immigrants are bad for the economy, any contact with an immigrant will be more negative than it would be if you harbored a positive belief.

Your beliefs also color any decision you make. If you believe that you are a poor person, your decision about purchases and investments will be different than it would be if you considered yourself wealthy or on the road to creating tangible wealth.

Finally, your beliefs also alter all actions you choose to take. If you believe you are a winner, your actions will be very different from those of a loser. To change your thoughts and actions, you must change your beliefs.

The Problem

You are probably aware of where I am heading with this. You are probably thinking that this system sounds too good to be true. To change your life, you simply create a new belief, such as "I am a wealthy person." Then your life will change, solutions will appear, the right things will happen, and you will suddenly be rich.

This would be perfect, except for one thing. Remember I mentioned that at about the age of eleven, your ability to change your beliefs easily stopped? Research has shown that the chemistry in your brain changed at that time. From that moment on, the brain connections that maintained your beliefs solidified. You began to find it more difficult to release old beliefs and accept new ones. By the time you reached adolescence, changing a belief became a major undertaking. Perhaps this is why there is truth to that old saying, "You can't teach an old dog new tricks."

As a result, your beliefs have a direct influence over all of your thoughts. When you receive new input that is in line with your beliefs, you welcome the input. Anyone associated with that input is viewed as being intelligent and supportive. Any organization or group associated with that input will appear to be wonderful.

But what happens when you hear something totally contrary to your present beliefs? You immediately become uncomfortable with that new idea. Your thoughts, based on your beliefs, automatically view this new idea with suspicion. You might assume that the source of the information is questionable. You then question the validity of what was given to you. If the source continues to push, you may start to oppose the idea.

Opposition to a pushy source with a new idea is swift. You may try to convince the other person to change his or her position. If you fail to accomplish that, you might then begin to argue with the person. Depending on how strongly you feel against the new idea and how dangerous it may be to your personal beliefs, you might finally go as far as to either ridicule or destroy the source of the new idea.

This is how most people act and interact in the world. They have so many strong beliefs, including religious, ethnic, cultural, sexual, and social beliefs. They also have regional and educational beliefs, as well as beliefs based on their language and local customs.

These general beliefs are not really a problem except when they interfere with the rights of others. The real problems with beliefs arise when people have strong beliefs on how to conduct business, politics, and relationships. The following are a few examples of beliefs that create problems:

"In business, the end always justifies the means."
"Management's job is to kick rear ends, so that people produce."
"I don't have an attitude problem, it's my personality."
"Computers? Who needs them?"
"This is the only way to run this organization."

These are just the tip of the iceberg. I am sure you can call up many other examples without much effort. This may come as a shock to some people, but most of their beliefs may not be accurate. In fact, studies indicate that at least 70 percent of the average person's beliefs are inaccurate. People have incorrect beliefs regarding every aspect of their lives, such as how they should treat people of a certain race, the best way to run a business, and which way the stock market is going for the rest of the year.

Why are so many of your beliefs incorrect? For one thing, the initial information you received may have been wrong. The messenger, sincere or otherwise, may have given you a distorted viewpoint, shared only a partial truth, or told you a lie.

Beliefs are also rendered obsolete by change. In our rapidly changing and evolving world, nothing remains the same. Remember, the half-life of information is less than five years and getting shorter. What was correct yesterday may be incorrect today. What is useful today may be useless by tomorrow. *To excel, you must be able to adapt and change your beliefs quickly.*

Right and Wrong Beliefs

Unfortunately, replacing your old beliefs with new ones is not an easy task. How can you determine which beliefs are correct and which are incorrect? Without this knowledge, you risk the possibility of accidentally discarding a valid and useful belief.

You can identify incorrect beliefs by looking at your life. If there is some aspect of your life that you do not like, it is probably the result of a wrong belief. The following are examples of a few limiting beliefs:

1. I am not wealthy.
2. It takes me forever to learn anything new.
3. I am not lucky.
4. I hate change.

If you are not wealthy and believe you will never be so unless you win the lottery, you own belief 1. If you find yourself resisting all efforts to learn how to use computers, you probably possess belief 2. If you do not like what you see in your own life, replace these limiting beliefs.

Changing Beliefs

To change your beliefs, you need a strategy. *Because the original beliefs were created by your thoughts, you need new thoughts to create new beliefs.* The following are a few examples:

1. I am wealthy.
2. I learn new things quickly.
3. I am lucky and always win.
4. I love change.

You must replace your old belief with your new belief. For instance, we can replace the commonly held belief, "I am not wealthy," with the new belief, "I am wealthy."

Destroying Old Beliefs

Change begins by tossing out the old belief. Begin by ridiculing or destroying all references that support your old belief of poverty. Listen to a few success stories, examples of others who have overcome their handicaps and succeeded.

This is the role of motivational speakers. They begin by telling people how bad things were for them. They may say, "I lost my legs in an accident," "I lost my eyesight overnight," or "I placed myself in incredible danger."

Then they describe how they overcame their difficulty or impossible situation. The message is clear. *If I can succeed, with my handicap or under the almost impossible odds I suffered, SO CAN YOU!*

The subconscious message that your subconscious mind concludes is this: "I am not suffering from that person's degree of handicap or difficulty. There is really no excuse for my not succeeding right now." The motivational speaker has placed a few holes in your old beliefs. He or she has opened the possibility for you to create a new belief: "I CAN DO IT, AND I CAN DO IT NOW!"

Finding Your New Beliefs

You can change any belief you desire. You simply have to identify the belief you want to have, and create it. To better understand which beliefs you want to change, ask yourself the following questions:

"Where do I want to be when I am sixty-five years old?"

"If I had already achieved my wish, what would I believe about myself?"

The answer to this question will help you to focus on what you want to become. Your belief has to be positive and phrased as if you were already living your new belief. In our example of having a lot of money, your belief might be the following:

"I am very wealthy."

When you have developed your new belief, you must repeat it to yourself both mentally and out loud. To be sure that your new belief enters your subconscious mind, use it in conjunction with several power techniques.

Adding Power

You can add strength to your affirmation by using four power techniques. These are repetition, authority, the support of others, and emotions.

Repetition

The first power technique is repetition. As you continually repeat your new belief, it is only a matter of time before you begin to believe it. Your constant repetition validates what you say. The more you repeat your new belief, the greater the effect it will have on you. With each repetition, the brain begins to solidify its channel connections for your new belief. *After about twenty-one days, the channel connection becomes solidified and permanent.*

Begin by mentally repeating to yourself, "I am wealthy," at least fifty times a day, every day. You can also repeat this aloud another fifty times a day. If you repeat this both mentally and aloud for a week, you will have said it to yourself seven hundred times. If you do it for a month, you will have done it over two thousand times. Before the end of the month, the channel connection is made.

Authority

The second power technique, authority, is the easiest to use. If you receive the approval of someone that you respect, you will probably believe that person immediately. It may take only a single statement from a recognized authority to turn an old belief around.

This is exactly what happened in my speaking career. I had already been speaking for more than fifteen years when I received an evaluation from a respected speaking coach. Until then, I really believed my speaking was not very good. Even when attendees complimented my speaking, their comments did not alter my low opinion.

When the speaking coach finally evaluated me, I was stunned. She suggested a few areas in which I could improve, but her overall opinion was very good. In fact, she placed me in the top section in more than half the categories. Needless to say, I was delighted.

From that moment on, I was a different speaker. Although I will always continue to work on honing my speaking and platform skills, my old belief that I was a lousy speaker has disappeared. I step on the platform with confidence. I truly see myself as a "professional speaker."

Change can happen as quickly as that. When someone you respect says something positive about you, your belief system changes immediately. If you continue to doubt yourself, the change will not take place.

Support of Others

The third power technique is the support of others. *If people support your efforts to change, you will have an easier time changing.* Supporters pick you up when you fall down. They motivate you with their encouragement and their "belief" in you. Behind every successful person are a lot of people who believed in that person.

This is how parents coax a child to walk. When the child first attempts to stand, a parent offers encouragement by saying, "Come on, you can do it. Come on, I know you can do it . . ."

The child takes a step, then falls down. The parent picks the child up and again coaxes him or her to walk. How long do the parents do this? As long as it takes for the child to walk.

Children need all the help they can get. After all, they are making a major paradigm shift. They are moving from the horizontal, crawling paradigm to the vertical, walking one. Without support, a child may decide that walking is just too difficult and crawling is good enough.

Making a major shift in your life is easier if, like a child, you have a lot of support. The last thing you need is a critic telling you, "You won't make it!" or "You failed before, and you'll fail again." You do not need anyone's help to fail. What you need are people who will support your efforts, whether you succeed or fall down. The more support you have, the greater your chances of success.

Emotions

The fourth and last power technique is the use of your emotions. Emotions are the power behind all beliefs. The stronger the emotion, the more likely a powerful belief will be formed.

The best emotion to use is a positive one. Positive emotions make this new belief feel more attractive. As discussed in the chapter on motivation, people are attracted to pleasure. If you can associate pleasure with your new belief, there is a greater likelihood that you will make this new belief permanent.

New Beliefs You Should Consider

The following are a few effective beliefs you should consider. If you do not yet have them, consider cultivating them:

"I'm open to new ideas and have a flexible mindset."

"I love to work with others in a team setting."

"I learn constantly and excel at my job."

"I'm in complete control of my attitude, and I keep it positive."

"I enjoy my life and everything in it."

"I love people and they love me."

As you build your new beliefs, support them with your actions. Act as if you are already there. If you believe that you are wealthy, you must think *and act* as if you were. If you are trying to believe you are thin and at your perfect weight, you have to act as if you were already there. *In life, repetition of an action eventually cultivates a habit and your habits become your new reality.* The next chapter will help you achieve this.

Step 3
Think Smart
(behavior)

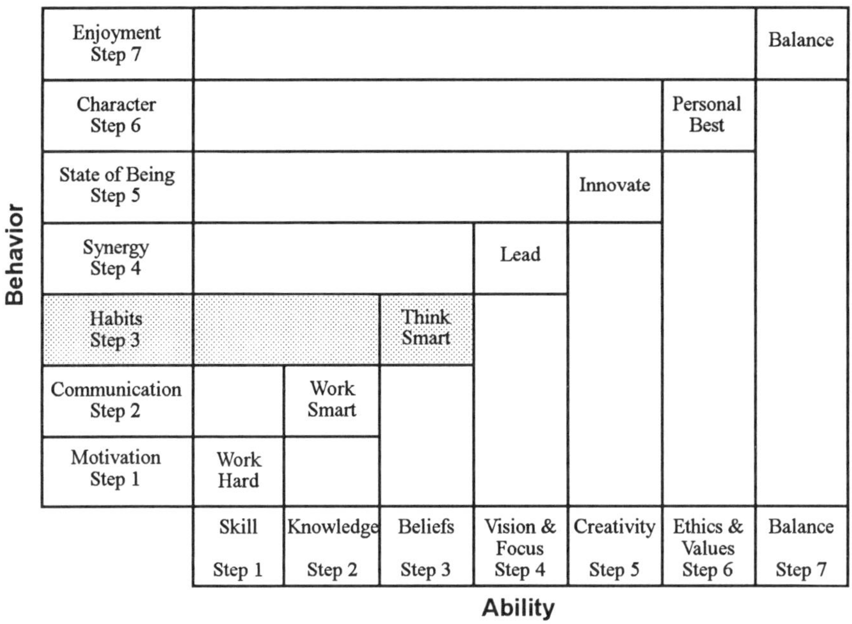

Chapter 8
Step 3: Think Smart (behavior)
Habits:
Creating Powerful New Habits

We are what we do repeatedly.
— Aristotle

Habits Are Beneficial

Habits are very powerful and useful mechanisms. They automate any action you perform repetitively. When you repeat anything over a period of time, your mind begins to memorize the sequence of actions. As is the case with your beliefs, three weeks of regular repetition create a habit. When a habit has been memorized, the mind no longer has to pay full attention to the sequence of actions. It can now concentrate on other tasks, making your life that much more efficient.

For instance, when you first learned how to drive a car, you had not yet acquired the habit of driving. The first time you sat behind the wheel of a car, your mind was probably overloaded with instructions. You had been told how to operate the clutch, brakes, gas pedal, and gearshift. You knew that somehow they were all supposed to work together. You were also told all of the rules of the road you had to follow. Filled with the theory of driving, you began.

You probably struggled the first time you drove on the road. Step-by-step, every movement of your hands and feet had to be thought out and executed. Although it was difficult at first, a few weeks of continuous practice eventually perfected the process. Soon the entire process became automatic.

After your driving habit is ingrained, you can repeat it without much conscious thought. It functions below your conscious awareness, in your subconscious mind. Your subconscious mind now handles the process of driving. Your conscious mind is now free to concentrate on other things, such as the scenery, your passengers, and your favorite music from your stereo.

Over your lifetime, you have probably developed habits for all of your common activities. You have different habits for a lot of standard activities at work, such as how to type on a computer screen, how to speak to certain people, what to do with a certain type of business form, or how to behave in a meeting. You also have habits for your golf swing, what you do after work, and how you speak to your children, spouse, or significant other.

Habits are a wonderful asset because they free your mind from the tedium of struggling to perform common repetitive activities. When habits are ingrained, they make your life so much easier.

How Habits Are Created

The relationships among your thoughts, actions, and habits are represented in the figure below:

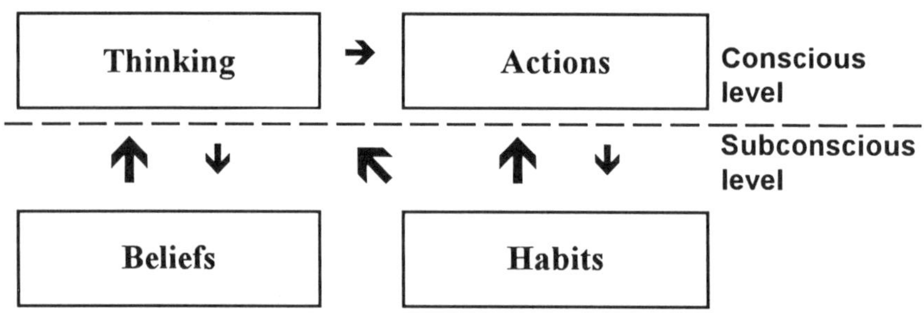

Figure 8-1: Interrelationship between Thoughts, Actions, and Habits

You have a thought of what you want to accomplish, and then you do it. This process is represented by a small arrow pointing from "thinking" to "actions." When the same actions is repeated, a habit is formed, which is also represented by another small arrow pointing from "actions" to "habits." After a habit is formed, it now begins to drive your actions and strongly influence your thoughts, which is represented by the large arrows pointing from "habits" towards "actions," and "thinking." Even without any thoughts, habits cause you to repeat your actions.

Habits Can Become a Problem

Life in momentum is wonderful, as long as nothing changes. Unfortunately, everything in your life is in the process of change. As changes occur in the world around you, some of your existing habits no longer serve any useful purpose. In fact, they may now hold you back. They push you to do what you have always done, not what you must do in order to excel.

As soon as an old habit becomes a liability, it is time to create a change. With training or education, you can learn what to do. Unfortunately, knowledge is often not enough. Even when you know what to do, you may find it impossible to make yourself actually do it.

I realized how difficult it was to change a habit when I had to drive an automobile in Japan. The people in Japan drive on the left side of the road and sit on the right side of the vehicle, as they do in England and Australia. As soon as I got behind the driver's seat, I felt uncomfortable. I was sitting on the "wrong" side of the vehicle and had to shift with my left hand. I rehearsed the shifting of the gears. Then, taking a deep breath, I started the car and drove down the street. It felt strange being on the wrong side of the street, but I soon thought I had the hang of it.

I simply followed the cars ahead of me. Everything was fine until I stopped at an intersection where I was the first driver in line. I was looking at a map and not paying attention to the traffic when the light turned. The horns from the cars behind me startled me as I quickly turned right. Suddenly I was heading toward the oncoming traffic and they began honking their horns at me. I panicked and stopped in the middle of the intersection. When I finally realized where I had to go, I slowly edged myself toward the left, where the other drivers were reluctant to let me in.

From that point on, I programmed myself for that situation. Before I made a right turn, I said to myself, "Stay on the left, stay on the left." In a matter of days, I was driving without thinking about my driving.

The difficulty I had in adapting to a new driving situation is the same difficulty everyone feels as they go through change. *If you are to excel in a changing environment, you must perfect the ability to change your habits.* To change your habits, you must understand how habits are created.

Changing a Habit

Most people try to change a habit through stubborn willpower. This "take the bull by the horns" technique is often frustrating. You know what to do, but you somehow cannot get yourself to do it. Faced with a constant uphill battle, most people eventually give up.

Why do people fail to change old habits, even when these old habits are bad for them? There are three basic reasons:

- Their beliefs do not support their new habit.
- They fail to create a new habit.
- They have the wrong associations with pleasure and pain.

New Beliefs

Changing an old habit begins with changing the beliefs that support the old habit. Without changing your beliefs, the process of change becomes laborious. *For change to be permanent, it must be an inside-out process. Until your beliefs change, outer changes are difficult.* You find yourself fighting the constant tendency to revert to your old ways. To create the beliefs that will support your new habits, follow the methods described in the previous chapter.

Creating a New Habit

The brain creates a habit through repetition. Just as beliefs were created with approximately twenty-one days of continuous repetition, habits require the same amount of time. Continuous repetition of the "right" actions will create the "right" habits.

Unfortunately, each time you backslide into the old habit pattern, you will reactivate that old brain connection. In a very short time, perhaps only a matter of seconds, the old connection will be alive and operational again. This is why you never forget the habit of riding a bicycle. Even if you have not ridden a bicycle in forty years, it usually takes only a few seconds before you are riding again.

To change a habit, this tendency to revert to the old must be stopped. This process can be helped with the right associations.

Associations for Pain and Pleasure

Creating a new habit is a change. As with all changes, you have to be motivated to create and maintain the change. To motivate yourself continually, you must associate pain with the old habit. This will motivate you to get out of the status quo of being "here." At the same time, you should associate pleasure with your new habit. Pleasure will motivate you to move to "there."

What kind of pain can you associate with the wrong habit? Suppose that you want to develop a habit of exercising every day. On the days that you fail, you can arrange for your family and friends to help you. When you forget to exercise, you can instruct them to stop you from having any dessert or watching any television programs. This association of pain with the wrong behavior can entice you remember to exercise.

What about controlling your temper? As soon as you realize that you have lost control and became upset, you can immediately go to the person you offended and get down on your knees. Then say to that person, "I am really sorry. Will you please forgive me? I promise to do my best never to do this again." Repeat this a few times, and you will naturally begin to change your ways.

Of course you should also reward yourself for the right action. If you maintain your exercise program or control your temper for a week, a great reward may be a professional massage or a simple pat on your own back.

Setbacks

Under stress or pain, you may have a tendency to revert to your old habits. There is a powerful reason that you do this. Deep in your subconscious mind, a lot of good and pleasurable memories are associated with your old habit. Stress tends to associate your present new activities with pain. Your subconscious mind concludes that the pain will go away if it reverts back to the old habit.

This is the reason that smokers revert to smoking and dieters quit their diets when under stress. When a smoker stops smoking or a dieter goes on a diet, there is a lot of pain associated with this action.

There was no pain when they were smoking or eating everything in sight. The subconscious mind wrongly concludes that returning to the old habit will end the pain. This does not have to happen to you.

Overcoming Setbacks

Where logic and reason fail, enough pain can overcome anything. People often come to me and ask, "I know what to do! My problem is I just can't seem to do it. What's going to get me to do it?"

My answer is simple. I ask them, "Is the pain bad enough yet?" When the situation people are in becomes painful enough, they seem to take action.

My father was once a heavy smoker. He said he knew he should quit smoking. He knew it was bad for his health. He was having problems breathing. It was making him feel sick, but he still found it impossible to quit.

As his health became progressively worse, he finally went to see his doctor. After examining him, the doctor told him he had to quit smoking. My father said he had tried so many times and failed. The doctor put it bluntly:

"Then I give you about a year, maybe two, to live. If you don't quit smoking, you'll be dead within two years."

That was the last day my father smoked. His fear (pain) of death was more than enough to overcome the addiction of smoking and the pain of quitting. For more than fifty years now, he has not smoked.

If you want to create a change, you do not have to wait until you are physically suffering. Instead, mentally associate enough pain with the old habit. Then associate enough pleasure with the new habit. *When the pain appears bad enough, and the pleasure feels good enough, you will be motivated to take the right action.*

Adding Energy

The statement, "Just do it!" rarely seems to be enough. You have to add power to your actions. It is all too easy to simply give up trying to create a change. You can add energy by using four energy-building tools: significance, emotions, visualization, and supporters.

Significance

The first energy-building tool is significance. Ask yourself, "Is this new habit important to the rest of my life?" If it is, it automatically gives you passion, energy, and determination. You receive a psychological boost from working toward something that is important to you.

If the new habit is not significant, you may be wasting your time. Why are you spending time on something that is not meaningful? Life is too short and time too precious to waste on unimportant things.

Emotions

The second energy-building tool, positive emotions, is a powerful supporter of change. When you are practicing your new habit, you have to express and maintain a strong, positive emotion. You must get really excited and feel good about your efforts. Feeling enthusiastic about yourself and your actions will associate pleasure with your new habit. It will also help to create a strong belief in your new habit.

Look at yourself in the mirror and yell, "Yes! You're the best," and feel it. Compliment yourself on all successes. This is not the time to be modest. Anything positive you can say or think about yourself will make you feel better and support your new habit.

Visualization

Visualization is the third energy-building tool. Mentally rehearse your new habitual actions. Research has shown that mental rehearsal is almost as good as actual practice. You see, your mind does not distinguish the difference between reality and your imagination. To the subconscious mind, they are nearly identical.

Take a moment and visualize yourself being "there." See yourself executing your new habit perfectly. If financial success is your goal, you must see yourself being successful. What does success mean to you? Picture yourself in the home you want to live in. See yourself in the type of automobile you want to be driving. Visualize yourself doing the things you wish to be doing when you are successful.

If your belief is to lose a certain number of pounds, visualize yourself being at your perfect weight. See yourself looking as you would look at that weight. Imagine yourself dressed in sleek clothing, going to parties, and dancing beautifully. Completely immerse yourself into being what you visualize.

Visualization is commonly used by a lot of athletes to prepare themselves for a perfect performance. They do it because they have experienced positive results from the practice. Visualization speeds the process of acquiring a new habit.

Supporters

Your supporters form the fourth energy-building tool. Your motivation remains high when those around you support your new efforts. The more supporters you have, the better your chances of success. Their positive outlook and understanding of your situation empower and continue to motivate you.

Supporters are powerful people in your life because you subconsciously seek approval from your peers. When you have supporters who are committed to helping you succeed, success comes easily. What would happen if someone were to recognize your accomplishments each time you moved in the right direction? What if each milestone you pass were applauded? Your supporters would bring pleasure to your being "there." They would actually be helping you to become the "new" you.

This is the basis for the power of support programs such as AA (Alcoholics Anonymous) and Weightwatchers. Each member understands what the others are going through. Great changes are possible when people support each other. If the group is able to create synergy, which we will discuss in a later chapter, magic happens.

What Habits to Change

Your habits create your future. To create a different future, you must carefully consider new habits to cultivate. You need the kind of habits that will create the future you truly desire. Consider adopting the following habits:

- Always be on time.
- Always do your best.
- Commit to helping others to succeed.
- Commit yourself to constant training and education.

- Remain self-motivated.
- Search and use creative solutions and ideas.
- Maintain a positive attitude.

Wisdom

I end this chapter by repeating one of my favorite sayings: *"Knowledge is what you know, wisdom is what you live."* The world is full of intellectual people. They have accumulated a great deal of knowledge about almost everything. Unfortunately, there are very few *wise* people. Become one of the wise ones by simply taking the best you have learned and living it. Applying any one of the principles contained in this book will increase your performance at work, as well as improve your personal life.

Step 4
Lead
(ability)

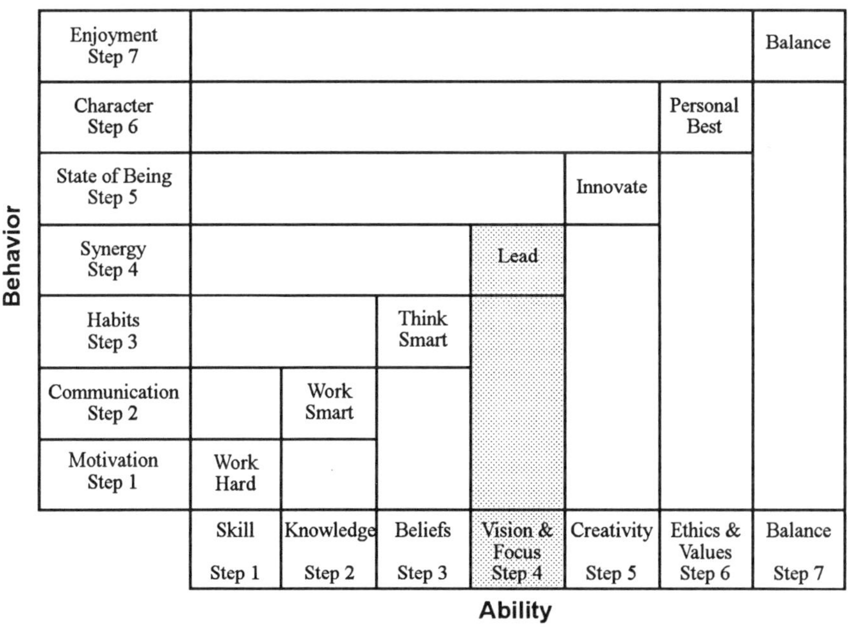

Chapter 9

Step 4: Lead (ability)

Vision and Focus: Creating Your Future

When a man does not know what port he is making for, no wind is the right wind. — Ralph Waldo Emerson

If you intend to go very far, you need a powerful vision to guide your life. Your vision is the ultimate goal you wish to attain in your life. It is at the very heart of why you do whatever you are doing. It is your purpose for living.

Actually, a vision is more of a dream than a goal. It is like a distant star, constantly pointing you in the right direction. It is the energizing factor that gets you motivated to do the right things at the right time.

Trying to live a life without a vision is similar to taking a trip without a destination in mind. How do you know that you are headed in the right direction? How do you decide which direction to turn? How will you know when you have arrived?

The Power of a Vision

Your present life is not an accident of nature. Your successes and failures did not just happen. Every decision you have ever made throughout your life had a part in creating the life you now lead. Every decision you make today will help to create your tomorrow. To obtain a new or different result, you must head in a different direction. You need a new vision.

If you pick a small vision, the results you create will be equally small. If you can allow your imagination to grow, you can develop a large vision. The larger your vision, the greater your results.

You must also feel passionate about your vision. It must have the power to motivate you into action, especially when you feel like doing nothing. It must be able to pick you up when you are feeling down.

After you have identified a powerful vision, making the right decisions becomes easy. Simply ask yourself, "Which way will take me closer to my vision?" One way usually stands out from the rest. That route is the right decision to make.

Naturally there will be times when you are tempted to waver from your vision. You must resist the temptation, or you will waste your most precious commodities: time and energy.

Just as your life was not an accident of nature, the attainment of professional power and personal excellence is not an accident. Achieving power and excellence is the result of methodical actions directed toward a far-away vision. You begin your journey by identifying your vision.

Identifying Your Vision

Obtaining a vision is a simple process. You just pick something and say, "This is my vision. This is where I want to go."

However, identifying a vision that is meaningful to you is much more difficult. It is a soul-searching process that will direct your life toward your highest aspirations, perhaps even your dreams.

Although finding and living your vision seems like a lot of work, the alternative is much worse. Living without a vision is similar to sailing a ship without a compass. Life can then reduce itself to a series of meaningless routines. Every day appears the same as any other day. Life becomes boring and time appears to accelerate because one day cannot be differentiated from another. Such a life can almost be reduced to a seven-step process: birth, growing up and education, work, marriage, parenting, old age, and death.

I remember when I first learned about the power of visions in the form of dreams. I found a quote by Marcus Aurelius, "What one man can dream, another can make real." I was so excited that I could hardly wait to get home and share this idea with my family. When my mother heard it, she added, "Yes, but first you have to have a dream."

My mother, in her quiet wisdom, blew me away. I needed a dream! I needed to know where I wanted to go. I needed a vision.

It was then that I decided that I wanted to become an electrical engineer. Becoming an engineer was really only a goal, but for a child growing up in a poor neighborhood in Hawaii, it was my vision. From that moment on, everything I did in school and at home was directed toward achieving that end. With my dream in mind, decisions were easy. I avoided things that pulled me away from my vision. I just did whatever I had to do to achieve my dream.

Creating a powerful vision is often a soul-opening task. *To discover your vision, you have to discover what you really want out of life.* You must put aside all of your doubts and fears to discover your dreams.

Before my speeches, I often send out questionnaires that ask attendees to share their visions. The most common answers I receive are the following:

Make a lot of money.
Retire or quit my job.
Raise my children well.

These are good goals, but they are not visions. Visions are much more than these. They are your highest aspirations.

Defining a Vision

Visions are much bigger than your goals. Goals are steps toward levels of achievement. They have a limited scope and are assigned a time frame for completion. Visions, on the other hand, are huge, almost eternal.

The following are some characteristics of a vision:

- A vision is large and powerful. It is your waking dream.
- A vision creates a picture image. The image is stored in the right brain and activated by feelings.
- A vision is altruistic. It is aimed at improving the world or creating an ideal situation.
- A vision is ethical, operating at the highest level of integrity.

- A vision creates passion, motivation, and dedicated action.
- A vision is simple and easy to remember.

Professional and Personal Visions

To begin to discover your professional and personal visions, you can play a simple visualization game. Close your eyes and visualize yourself at your own retirement party. You are seventy years of age because the retirement age has been pushed up. All of your friends and relatives are there with you, congratulating you on your retirement. Your co-workers are also there congratulating you. Ask yourself the following questions:

- "What have I really accomplished in my professional life?"
- "What have I accomplished in my personal life?"
- "Have I accomplished everything I thought I would?"
- "What do members of my family say about me?"
- "What do my friends say about me?"
- "What does society say about me?"
- "Am I really happy about where I am?"

From the answers you have recorded, form a mental image of what your life has been. The image you see is probably a mental projection based upon your present life path. This image is an older version of where you are now headed if you make no significant changes in your life. To move out of your present mindset, ask yourself these questions:

- "Is this everything I really wanted to accomplish?"
- "What more would I really have wanted to accomplish?"
- "What do I want my family to say about me?"
- "What do I want my friends to say about me?"
- "What do I want society to say about me?"

To discover your vision, ask yourself the following questions:

- "What do I love to do?"

- "What do I do that really excites me?"
- "What do I do without getting paid?"
- "If money was not a limitations, what would I have done?"
- "What would I just love to accomplish if I could not fail?"

Your answers to these questions are probably very close to your vision. This is probably where your real passion lies. This is something that you would love to do more than anything else. It is what you truly want to achieve in your life.

Now you can take your answer and push it to its ultimate conclusion. Make it a grand ideal that you may never reach. Test your vision to see if it is good enough:

- Is my vision simple and easy to remember?
- Does my vision create a picture image?
- Is my vision altruistic?
- Is my vision ethical?
- Does my vision create passion and motivation?
- Am I willing to sacrifice for my vision?

When you have selected your vision, you can use it to guide you for now. At some future time, perhaps in a couple of weeks, you can repeat the exercise. Redefining your vision can be a lifetime process.

Consider these two great professional visions:

> *One person, one computer.* Steve Jobs and Steve Wozniak, Apple Computer.
>
> *I will be the world's greatest inventor.* Thomas A. Edison.

These are powerful visions. They meet all of the tests for a vision. They are bigger than the people who created them. Steve Wozniak and Steve Jobs did not achieve their vision but took a lot of us on a wonderful and exciting journey. Thomas Edison achieved his vision in his lifetime and made the world a better place in which to live.

You may not have such a grand vision. You may never achieve your vision. But that does not mean that you should not have one. We all need a vision to guide our lives and create our destinies.

My Visions

At one time, my professional vision was *Motivate and empower 100 million people to achieve professional excellence and personal enjoyment.* I have modified this vision over the years. For one thing, I did not want to limit myself to 100 million people. I may be reaching that figure soon. (Remember, think BIG!)

I also wanted people to have more than professional excellence. I wanted them to have power. In their personal lives, I felt they needed more than enjoyment. I wanted them to have excellence. Thus my current professional vision is, *Empower, motivate, and educate people to achieve excellence.*

This is my present vision. Tomorrow it may be different, but this is the direction in which I am now headed. This is what excites me. This is the true reason I get up in the morning. It is my wish to make everyone the best they can become.

My personal vision appears to be different from my professional one. I want to achieve three basic qualities in my life: *love, joy, and peace of mind.* These are the qualities I seek in my own life. Everything I do is an attempt to achieve more love, joy, and peace of mind in my life.

Naturally there are times when the pursuit of my personal vision conflicts with the attainment of my professional one. In those cases, I usually try to make a choice based on my personal vision. I try not to chase after my professional vision at the price of my personal one.

To achieve professional power and personal excellence, your professional and personal visions should agree, as much as possible, with each other. In my case, helping people to succeed gives me tremendous joy. It makes me feel good to see people gain an insight on how to improve their lives. *When your professional and personal visions are in alignment, you will have tremendous power.*

Finally, it would be ideal if your professional and personal visions also agreed with the vision of the organization you work for. When the organization's vision agrees with your visions, you can commit yourself to your work. With agreement, you develop passion. However, if your visions are in conflict with that of your organization, commitment and passion may not be possible. It then becomes very difficult to perform at levels of excellence.

Organization's Vision

My wife once worked as the assistant to the director of a small but rapidly growing mail-order company. The company sold products that helped people to improve their personal lives. Their advertised purpose was to help people.

This seemingly visionary company attracted people who also wanted to help others. They had one of the most dedicated groups of employees working for them. The employees loved to extend themselves beyond the call of duty.

Over the period of a couple of years, however, the executives displayed their true intent. Perhaps they started with a sincere interest to help others, but in the end, they were simply in it for the money. Their advertised purpose was only a marketing angle. They were not living the message they were presenting.

When these idealistic employees discovered this, it really offended them. They felt deceived. Several quit. Others continued working there, but their hearts were no longer in their work. A few felt vengeful toward the company.

Mark Shepherd, past chairman of Texas Instruments, has said that it is not the leaders that move an organization to greatness, but the organization's dream. Each individual is subordinate to the organization's vision.

Today many organizations are getting on the "vision" bandwagon, flying their vision for everyone to admire. Yet most of the visions I have seen are nothing more than mission statements. They neither excite nor guide people toward an organization's ultimate destination.

As if this were not bad enough, many organizations do not practice what they claim. They say, "We value our people," and they do not. They say, "We value our customers," and they fail to do so. They may even say, "We're green," and their environmental claims may be skewed. For them, having a great vision is simply a marketing tool, something to show off to prospective clients and concerned stockholders. It excites neither management nor employees. Their advertised vision is a window dressing hiding a dirty store.

To be a useful tool, an organization's vision must be authentic. It must not be simply a marketing strategy or a way to appease stockholders. When employees and stockholders discover that they have been fooled, they become angry and vindictive.

When an organization's vision is authentic, it aligns employees who are committed to the same vision. When there is alignment, there is dedication and loyalty. People are inspired to attain the organization's vision.

Your Organization's Vision

If people are to align with the organization's vision, they need to know what it is. Does everyone know the organization's vision? Most people do not.

Before many of my presentations, I take a survey of employees, managers, and executives. I ask them what, in their own words, is their organization's vision. Most of them do not have a clue. Some will attach the organization's mission statement. The remainder give a lot of different and sometimes conflicting ideas. It is very obvious how really unimportant their organization's vision is when no one can remember what it is or where to find it.

If your organization does not have a vision, it is time to create one. The best way to develop a vision is to form a focus group. Have various people from within your organization meet to develop a common vision. To help you develop your organization's vision, ask yourself the following questions:

- Does this vision excite people?
- Is it in line with the culture we wish to develop?
- Is this vision simple and easy to remember?
- Does this vision create a picture image?
- Is this vision ethical?
- Does this vision create passion and motivation?
- Am I willing to sacrifice for this vision?

When you have developed your organization's vision, your must let everyone know what it is. You can publish the organization's vision in every copy of the newsletter. You can have it printed on a laminated pocket card for every employee to carry or on the back of all identification cards. You can post it on every bulletin board.

When employees align with an organization's vision, people are willing to commit to that organization. To sustain that commitment, organizations must also commit themselves to the employees.

Take a moment and ask yourself the following question: "Does my organization's vision agree with my personal and professional visions?" If it does not, you are probably in the wrong business or working for the wrong reasons. You should seriously consider changing your job or career.

Bringing Your Vision Down To Earth

To make your vision practical, you must develop a practical, step-by-step plan. You can achieve this by using your vision to create your goals, priorities, obstacles, strategies, tactics, plan, and schedule.

Goals

Once you have established your professional and personal visions, list the goals you need to move yourself in the direction of your vision. Goals are your signposts, indicating where you want to be and when you want to get there.

Remember, your vision tends to remain the same. In my case, one of my visions is to maintain joy in my life. Although my vision of joy will remain the same, the goals I use to attain this vision will change from year to year.

Suppose that one of your visions, also, is to attain as much joy as possible. You must establish goals that will help you to enjoy your life. For instance, suppose that your goals for the next year are these:

Take a two-week vacation in Hawaii.
Purchase a new car.
Read at least one new book a month.
Visit my folks for a week.

Priorities

After you have established your goals, you must create priorities. List your goals in their order of importance. Then record the date by which you wish to achieve each goal. The list above now becomes the following:

1. Visit my folks for a week by September 30.
2. Take a two-week vacation in Hawaii in December.

3. Read at least one new book a month starting now.
4. Purchase a new car in June.

Obstacles

With every goal, list the obstacles that prevent you from achieving that goal. Ask yourself the following questions:

What resources do I lack in order to achieve this goal?

Does anyone or anything stand in my way?

What has to happen to achieve my goal?

Who could help me achieve my goal?

Strategies and Tactics

After you have identified your obstacles, you can devise strategies to overcome them. If you lack funds, you must devise a method to obtain more funds. If you lack time, you must find a creative method to free up more time.

Your strategy is an overall concept of how you are going to overcome the obstacles that prevent you from achieving your goals. Your tactics are the step-by-step methods you will use to achieve the goals. The following is a simple example:

My goal: Take a two-week vacation in Hawaii.

My obstacles: Lack of vacation time. I need four extra days.

My strategy: Work on weekends for others, so they can cover for me.

My tactics: Contact my co-workers immediately so we can make the proper arrangements. I will trade two days with Jack, and two days with Helen.

Plan of Action and Schedule

A plan of action should never be a detailed document. It should be as short and as simple as possible. You should be able to adapt your plan quickly as changes occur in your life.

The following is an example of a plan of action:

Work for Jack on March 3 and July 3.

Work for Helen on April 15 and 22.

Take my vacation in mid-September.

You can see that your goals, priorities, plans, and schedule grow naturally out of your visions. Your visions guide your professional and personal lives.

Focus

Once you have established your vision, goals, and plans, you must focus your energies in the direction of your top-priority goals. The greater your ability to focus on achieving your highest-priority items, the more power you give yourself.

Your ability to focus on what is important is also called time management. Your ability to get others to focus on attaining certain results is called leadership.

To manage your time, you must focus your energies on your top-priority goals. With this kind of focus, decision-making becomes so much easier. All decisions take you either closer to or further from your goal. Whenever a decision is required, simply ask yourself, "Will this help me to achieve my goal?"

The answer is usually yes, no, or maybe. If the answer is yes and the action sounds economically and otherwise feasible, you should implement the decision. If the answer is maybe or no, throw the idea out. This tool is especially valuable when your are faced with tough decisions. Ask yourself the question and then follow the choice that leads you closer to your top-priority goals. If any decision takes you away from your goal, you must be willing to say, "No, I don't need that."

Leadership is your ability to focus other people's energies to attain the desired results. You begin by sharing your vision with everyone. You then help them to maintain their focus on achieving the correct results. As a leader, you can guide people's actions by doing the following:

1. Establish a clear vision for the people you lead. It does not matter whether you are the head of a team, a department, a division, or the entire organization; you must have a clear vision for people to follow. Without vision, people tend to continue doing what they have always done, or else head off on a tangent.

2. Set an example of the behavior desired. As a leader, you must "walk the talk." You must be able to continually demonstrate the behavior you desire from the people you lead. Remember that at every moment, people are watching what you are doing. Everything you say, believe, value, and

reward is being interpreted throughout the organization. They are watching to see how you behave, especially under stressful times. If you fail, you will lose much of your credibility.

3. Realize that your ultimate task is to increase human energies. The people you lead have only their energy and knowledge to give. Your job is to maximize their energy and knowledge, and then direct them where they will accomplish the necessary results.

4. Remove obstacles that people face. Leaders must address obstacles and take action to remove them.

5. Support innovation and creativity. Innovative and creative ideas are resident in everyone. Your task as a leader is to bring these out and support them. We will discuss innovation and creativity in Chapter 12.

As you focus on your visions, your decisions will all be pointed in the right direction. With the right decisions, you will begin to create the future you desire. Today is the result of yesterday's decisions, and tomorrow will be the result of the decisions you make right now. *While your large decisions seem to be the major influence in your life, it is the daily small decisions you make that have the greatest impact on your life.*

In my case, my professional vision makes me focus on my speaking. It has my highest priority. Right behind that is the writing of this book. Whenever there is a short break from my speaking schedule, I concentrate my efforts on finishing this book.

At the time of this writing, another high-priority item is to upgrade my presentation through the use of multimedia computer systems. To achieve this, I have purchased a new multimedia, laptop computer. I now have the right software and have given numerous presentations using my computer.

Although vision and focus are important, your ability to lead and to create the life you desire is greatly influenced by your ability to work with others. In the following chapter, you will learn how to create synergy, the ultimate in teamwork.

Step 4
Lead
(behavior)

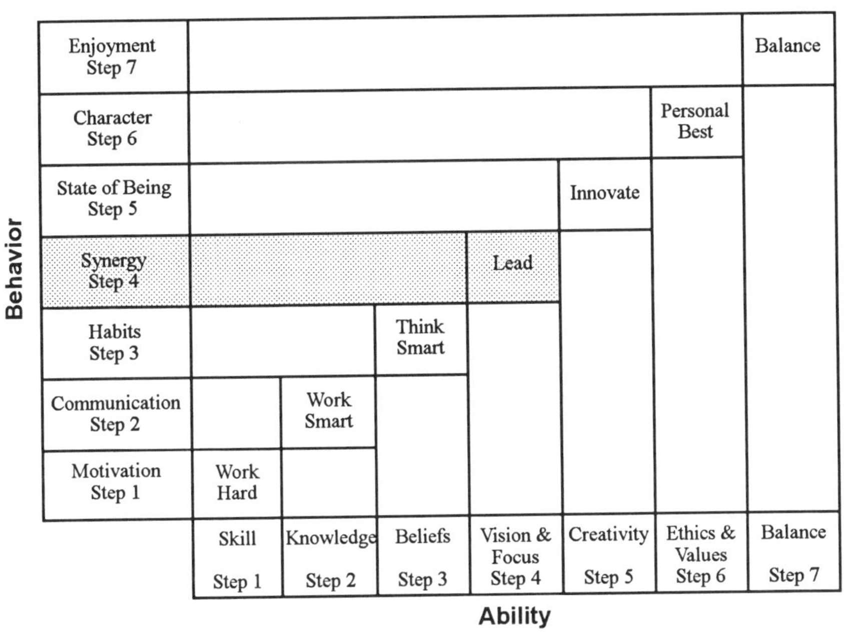

Chapter 10
Step 4: Lead (behavior)
Synergy: The Ultimate In Teamwork

It's easy to get good players. Getting them to play together, that's the hard part. — Casey Stengel

Synergy is defined as the ability to work together. I would like to expand that definition to this: *Synergy is a state of tremendous cooperation in which the group's achievements are greater than the sum total of each individual working alone.*

It was very early in my engineering career that I first became aware of the phenomenon of synergy. One morning, my supervisor called me in to discuss the reinstallation of a critical communications system. As he outlined what I had to do, I kept a mental estimate of how long this project would require, according to our "normal" timetable. When he finished, my mental total was about a month, maybe a little longer. If this was a "real" emergency, I could probably do it in two weeks.

I then asked him, "How long do I have to complete this project?" I should have seen it coming when he raised his arm and glanced down at his watch. My face sagged when he replied, "You have exactly twenty-eight hours to do this. The system has to be operational by tomorrow noon!"

Hiding my shock, I confidently replied, "No problem! I'll be done by then."

It was only then that reality and fear set in. You see, until that moment, I had never actually installed any communications equipment, much less a whole system. As a design engineer, I had drawn a lot of plans for installing various types of equipment and systems, but I had not yet touched any "real" equipment. For the first time, I would have to put my hands where my drawing pencil had always been.

With Mits Fukushima, an outstanding veteran technician, to assist me, we started to collect everything we thought we would need. I found a copy of the old installation plans and studied the system. We then went to the organization's warehouse and borrowed, openly or covertly, all of the components and installation material we estimated we would need. When we finally arrived at the site, we found the system needing greater work than my supervisor had described.

The two of us were determined to complete this job on schedule. After all, our reputation was at stake. Well, at least Mits' reputation was at stake. You see, up to this point, I had no reputation for installing equipment, but I knew I would certainly have one if we could not make this system work! Working as fast as we could, we studied the problem, created a plan of action, divided the work, and charged ahead.

We both remained focused on what we wanted to accomplish. We worked together when a single person could not do the job. As we worked, I began to sense something different. There was a silent feeling of camaraderie, and I knew something special was happening. I did not feel tired, and I did not feel any hunger pangs. The longer we worked, the more energized I felt.

Eleven long hours later, the system was fully operational. We had completed that job in less than half the time we were given. More importantly, we had actually completed what we had both estimated to be at least a month's job in a single, long working day.

I fondly remember that project even now. In my mind, it was one of those enjoyable and almost magical moments. Even Mits has commented about it periodically, about how great it was to have worked together. There was a wonderful synergy between the two of us. This experience between Mits and me was never repeated.

As soon as we returned to the office, we fell back into our usual routine. It seemed as if nothing special had ever happened. Even when we received a letter of commendation for our efforts, I simply stuffed that piece of paper into my personal folder and quickly forgot about it. Every following job took just as long as it had before that emergency job, and I worked at the same methodical pace I had been accustomed to. I never even wondered what had made that project so special.

Although the experience was never repeated with Mits, I have experienced the same synergic state on numerous occasions with many other people. I never really concerned myself about synergy until I became a part of management. As a manager, I realized that if we could all work together, just as Mits and I had done that day, productivity would increase dramatically.

Synergy Is Common, but Spotty

I discovered that operating in synergy, at greatly elevated performance levels, is not uncommon. At my speeches and seminars, many attendees say that they have experienced something similar, or that they have heard similar stories from others. This means that nearly everyone is capable of working in synergy. This natural phenomenon occurs in every field, from manufacturing to sports, insurance to military operations. You may have similar stories to share.

Unfortunately, most people seem to rise to peak performance levels only when they are experiencing an emergency or are under an urgent deadline. Ron, a fellow engineer in another department, had a similar occurrence when he was in Antarctica. Ron's team's departure was delayed because of equipment shipment delays. When the equipment was shipped and his team finally arrived in Antarctica, they were months behind schedule.

Speaking with the person in charge about their schedule, Ron was shocked when they were told, "You must complete your installation in two weeks."

"Impossible!" exclaimed Ron. "There is no way we can finish this job in less than two months. By the way, why do we have to finish in two weeks?"

"Because the last ship leaves here in two weeks. If you're not on that ship, you're wintering over. The next ship will be arriving in about seven or eight months from now."

At that moment, the whole team understood. They really had only two weeks to complete the job. They started working immediately. Everyone did their best, helping each other to complete their tasks.

The usual complaining was held to a minimum. When they were too tired to continue working, some of them even slept alongside the equipment. When they got up, they immediately began working again. Motivation was never a problem. In two weeks, the job was completed and the whole team was aboard the last ship home.

People seem to create synergy naturally when they experience great stress or are in an emergency situation. They often experience synergy while in a battle, fighting a common foe. Synergy sometimes occurs when people come together for the common good, as in an environmental movement or under a Mahatma Gandhi. What more could you accomplish if there were a way to create the conditions that make synergy possible?

Creating Synergy

Synergy is not a state that can be forced. Rather, it seems to happen by itself, when the right conditions exist. What can you do to create the environment that promotes synergy? Synergy seems to flourish under the following conditions:

1. Powerful vision or purpose
2. Supportive and sharing culture
3. Positive viewpoint

Powerful Vision or Purpose

The most important factor in creating synergy is a common vision that energizes people. You must have a powerful purpose to pull people together. Your vision or purpose has to be large enough that people will set aside their petty differences to work toward attaining the group's vision.

For example, the vision could be the prevention of organizational cutbacks or downsizing. It could be the creation of a breakthrough product or the overcoming of a great problem. It could just as well be the group's desire to develop a new procedure or a new recipe for a chocolate dessert.

However, a powerful vision alone is usually not enough to magically transform a group of people into a synergic group. There will always be a lot of skeptics who resist joining in. It is a leader's job to convert these people, one at a time. Leaders must get people to "buy into" the common vision.

At some point, somewhere between 30 and 40 percent, a group seems to reach critical mass. Suddenly, everyone is "on board" or into the program and moving toward the common goal. Because critical mass usually requires between a 30 and 40 percent "buy-in," synergy is easier to achieve in smaller groups.

Often synergy is easier to create with a negative stimulus. When a group is confronted by a common enemy or is facing a dangerous situation, it is easier to build synergy. On the battlefield, for instance, a powerful synergy always seems to exist among soldiers fighting for their lives. This same synergic state can exist in a medical team performing an especially difficult surgery or in a drug company laboratory team trying to produce a lifesaving drug.

Supportive Culture

A supportive culture also helps to make synergy possible. In a supportive group, people work together and play together. They develop a bond, a feeling of camaraderie. They are creating a win/win situation, in which everyone has the possibility to win.

Real synergy is developed in the corporate world when people begin sharing ideas with each other. Unfortunately, this can be difficult in a "me-focused" society such as that in the United States, where each person wants to hoard secrets to protect his or her position. Individuals have to understand the benefits of sharing. If each person in a group could share one idea, no one would be less for it and everyone would be better. As creative ideas and approaches are shared, the effectiveness of the group is greatly enhanced. Suddenly everyone is better. There is no way of explaining it. When each person is driven by a powerful vision in a supportive culture, "magic" sometimes happens.

In sports the building of synergy is sometimes called "coming together" or "jelling." When synergy is attained, it is sometimes called "being in the zone." When a group is in the zone, everyone becomes outstanding. Nothing can stop them. Everything they do is right, if not almost perfect.

The individuals who comprise the group also develop a pride in themselves. They feel that they are the best, that they can accomplish anything. A positive attitude, with a little pride, goes a long way in creating a supportive culture.

Positive Viewpoint

In the process of creating synergy, the group must stop looking at problems as problems. Instead, they must try to see all problems as challenges over which they can triumph. To the synergic group, nothing is impossible. They must be confident in their abilities and be able to support each other. They must also be able to maintain a positive state of being, always focused on solving problems or attaining positive results. We will discuss how to create and maintain a positive state of being in later chapters.

Critical Mass

When critical mass is achieved and synergy is established, motivation is almost automatic. You feel ready to contribute to the completion of any task with which the group is faced. Your mindset suddenly changes from "me" to "we." Also, any win/lose mentality changes to win/win. At this point, reluctance tends to become cooperation, and suspicion tends to become trust. Problems and difficulties actually energize the group.

Until critical mass is attained, you must foster conditions that allow the formation of synergy. As a leader, you should attempt to build a sense of caring, in which everyone is concerned with everyone else's success. An environment of cooperation will go a long way to building that sense of caring.

You must also communicate a sense of trust. You can achieve this by trusting all members of the group and trusting that they will succeed. Establish trust by holding the group accountable for the desired results.

There are no real hard-and-fast rules guaranteeing that a group will experience synergy, but by following the three guidelines given above, your chances of creating and experiencing synergy will increase. When synergy occurs, the group's creativity and productivity will skyrocket to unbelievable levels!

Negative Synergy

You must constantly guard against negative synergy, which is surprisingly pervasive. Negative synergy is created when an individual or several individuals become self-serving. They try to boost themselves by putting others down. They create win/lose situations instead of helping everyone create a win/win situation. They also tend to develop a culture that runs down or belittles others for mistakes or failures.

The signs of negative synergy are easy to spot. Morale and productivity both decline. Complaints and bickering increase. When you see this happening, you must take immediate action to improve the work environment. Remember that old saying, "If things are not getting better, they're probably getting worse."

Creating positive synergy may sound like a lot of work, but it is worth the effort. When such synergy is created, the general work environment becomes more satisfying. Performance and productivity increase more than a few percentage points. They may actually rise by one hundred or more percentage points!

Until synergy emerges, leaders must motivate people. The next chapter provides effective methods for building continuous motivation.

Chapter 11
Step 4: Lead (behavior)
Motivation: Motivating Others

I have found enthusiasm for work to be the most priceless ingredient in any recipe for success. — Samuel Goldwyn

Art of Leadership

In today's increasingly complex environment, no one succeeds alone. At some point, just about everyone is placed in a position of leadership. Whether you are an employee, corporate executive, or parent, success comes only when you enlist the assistance of as many people as possible. *As a leader, your primary job is to help others become a success.*

As discussed earlier, success (performance) is dependent on two factors: ability and behavior. Most people generally know what to do. If they do not, it is easy to provide them with that information. What most people lack is the motivation to do what they know they should do. A leader's problem is generally one of motivating people.

In any leadership role, your primary interaction with the people you lead is to motivate them to move from "here" to "there." In fact, one of the most important keys to management success is your ability to motivate others. Lee Iacocca said, "Management is nothing more than motivating people." He realized that people knew how to do their jobs. Their problem was getting themselves into gear and actually performing.

Unfortunately, most leaders do not have an effective motivational strategy. The methods they use are often the same methods that were used on them. Sometimes they hear what others in their field are doing to motivate their people and decide to imitate that behavior. When they fail to achieve the results they desire, they either blame the person who gave them the idea or else claim that their people were beyond hope.

Just as you may sometimes find it difficult to motivate yourself, other people are suffering from the same problem. They automatically resist making any changes to their lives. When they get into a comfortable pattern that seems to work, they tend to continue doing the same thing. They create a comfort zone of behavior that others find almost impossible to penetrate.

I have two very close friends in Hawaii who came to visit me in Arizona. Helen and her husband are both highly qualified professionals who had recently retired. They wanted to get involved in something to keep themselves busy and also to make some extra money. We spent a lot of time investigating various options. By the end of the second day, the three of us had created a great plan of action. They were excited and motivated to put their plan into action as soon as they returned to Hawaii.

A few weeks after they left, I called them to see how they were progressing.

"Helen," I asked, "how are you doing with your new venture?"

"Oh," she sighed, "we're not doing too much."

"What happened?"

"Well, you know how it is. When we got back to Hawaii, we got polynesian paralysis."

We had a good laugh. However, "polynesian paralysis" is not limited to the Hawaiian Islands. It occurs everywhere. As soon as people return to their familiar environment, they quickly fall back into their comfortable, habitual routines. Work, family responsibilities, and social obligations quickly fill all their time. In a short while, they have lost the motivation they acquired. This experience made me aware that if motivating others is going to work, it has to be part of an intelligent strategy that is consistently applied over a long period of time.

Random Motivation

Motivation is an essential ingredient in altering and guiding people's behavior. If you want to entice other people to improve their behavior, you need a coherent plan to motivate them. However, even managers, who are supposed to be professional motivators, do not have a consistent plan to motivate their people. In fact, many managers have no plan at all.

I recently had to facilitate a session for a group of sales managers. In it, I asked the attendees what motivational techniques they used to motivate their people. Their answers included:

"I kick butt."

"We have an incentive plan. More sales, bigger percentage of commission."

"We give top performers an incentive trip."

"I give out awards."

"Nothing."

Although they gave different answers, each answer was a form of either pain or pleasure. Most of these actions will affect people's behavior. Depending on the group and the individuals within that group, these actions will create different results. I then asked, "Does it work consistently? Why does it or does it not work?"

I heard a lot of murmuring and grumbling. The consensus was that it sometimes worked, and only on certain individuals. It was clear that they really did not understand how to motivate others. To them, motivation was a hit-or-miss game. Sometimes their techniques really seemed to work. Other times they fell flat. If you are going to motivate others consistently, you have to understand the various types of motivators and how to use them effectively.

A Motivation Plan

Most efforts to motivate another person are short-term motivation. Like you, other people are motivated by pain, pleasure, and the price of change. To persuade others to change, you can create a simple four-part plan of action:

1. Identify the desired "there."
2. Motivate out of "here" with pain.

3. Identify the reward or pleasure they will receive when they arrive "there."
4. Lower the price of change.

Identifying the Goal

Before trying to motivate anyone into action, you must begin with a clear goal in mind. What is it that you are trying to achieve? *Unless the people you are trying to motivate know exactly what they are suppose to achieve, they may end up doing the wrong thing.*

Ask yourself: What do I want the other person to do? If you are trying to increase the bottom line of sales, make that clear to your people. Otherwise, they may think that you want them to increase the number of sales they make. They might then make more sales at lower prices which would fail to improve the bottom line. Communicate your needs clearly. To be sure that you have, ask people for feedback.

Here is a common example of an unclear goal: A government facility was about to have an inspection. Being in the middle of a heavy workload, the facility was a mess, with boxes, forms, and reports scattered on test benches. The manager told the workers, "We're having an inspection tomorrow afternoon, and this place is a mess. It needs to be organized. Clean it up by tomorrow morning. I want this place looking sharp."

The technicians quickly began doing as they were told. The empty boxes were neatly piled in one corner. The strewn paperwork was piled on each test bench in separate piles for each item being worked on.

The manager returned early the next morning and was not happy with the results. He began shouting, "I told you to get rid of the boxes, throw them out. And do the same thing with all the paperwork. Hide them in the file cabinets. Now get this place in shape by noon."

The manager then stormed off, upset with everyone. The technicians were also upset. Morale was down as they begrudgingly did what they were ordered to do. This situation could have been prevented if the manager had told the technicians exactly what he wanted from them. The manager failed to communicate the exact result he desired and also failed to recognize their efforts as "cleaning it up."

Before you try to motivate people, clearly identify the results you want. Ambiguous statements such as "Just do it better" will probably not give you the results you desire.

Motivating with Pain

The purpose of using pain is to persuade people to push out of "here," out of their comfort zone. The following is a list of pain motivators, listed in order of increasing severity:

1. Ask the person to change something.
2. Give a verbal reprimand in private.
3. Threaten to give a low evaluation.
4. Threaten to take away one or more privileges.
5. Give a low evaluation.
6. Take away one or more privileges.
7. Threaten to reduce pay or demote the person.
8. Ridicule in public.
9. Reduce pay or demote the person.
10. Threaten to terminate the person.
11. Terminate the person as an example to others.

When using pain, be careful to use only as much pain as necessary to achieve the desired results. If you go too high on the list, you are probably using too much pain. Instead of motivating that person, you will probably incite a reaction. The greater the pain experienced, the more negative the reaction. In fact, if enough pain is used, the reaction may become hostile.

The possible reactions by employees are listed in increasing order:

1. Work harder until you turn your back.
2. Question everything you say.
3. Give lots of excuses.
4. Complain about things that hold them back.
5. Fail to inform you of problem areas.

6. Make you look bad or foolish, and do it covertly.
7. Make life difficult for you.
8. React with verbal violence or lies.
9. React with physical violence.

Managers generally misinterpret the reactions of people. When workers begin to exhibit reactions 1 through 5, managers assume that they have an attitude problem. They then react by trying to motivate the workers with even more pain. Over time, the reactions escalate and may eventually result in physical violence.

By the time a person reacts violently, there is a problem deep within the entire department or organization. Violence is the "final straw." People usually tolerate a lot of threats and abuse from their supervisor and co-workers. They tend to stash their frustration and anger inside, allowing it to build slowly over time. Finally, when the pain gets to a point that they can no longer contain it, they explode. They often react by quitting. In a few cases, they may resort to violence and attack the source of their pain.

Remember that even the best of intentions can provide the wrong results. Mike, an employee in a software company, shared this horror story with me. His company had many offices in separate locations. Because of declining sales, management had to take action quickly. The company decided to begin cutbacks to reduce expenses and improve their bottom line. The cutbacks reduced morale, which in turn reduced productivity. Over a period of time, not only did morale not improve, it actually got worse. Observing the situation, Mike attributed the decaying morale and productivity to a single person, the human resource person who visited the various sites on Fridays.

Every Friday, for about an hour, everyone in every branch office kept an eye on the front walkway. As Mike put it, ". . . and if that witch came walking up the walkway wearing black, at least one person at that office was going to be fired that day." When she came in wearing black, everyone in that branch office tensed. Then they waited, like desperate prisoners, praying that today was not going to be their day of execution.

The human resource person was deliberately doing this to send a message to everyone in the company. Her intended message was probably, "Here's another person (or several people) who did not measure up. You had better shape up or I'll ship you out, too." She wanted more motivated people, people with better performance and higher productivity. Unfortunately, the results she created were the exact opposite. She was single-handedly sending motivation and productivity into the gutter. How? She threatened people's very survival. For many people, existence is almost a hand-to-mouth operation. Their job is the only safety net that keeps them off the streets. By threatening people's livelihood, she lowered performance, productivity, and profit margins.

This is not to imply that corporations should not create change through mergers, layoffs, or downsizing. But during and after the change, the heads of corporations should expect worker's enthusiasm to wane. When motivation drops, they must take immediate action to resurrect it.

Yet I hear from many executives and managers who are puzzled as to why morale and motivation drops after a personnel cutback. They think people should be "professionals" and just pull themselves up by their bootstraps. Some managers not only want people to carry on as if nothing had happened, they also expect people to become even more motivated and productive. More often than not, they also expect the remaining employees to absorb the work of the missing people. This is a new twist on the old joke that goes, "The beatings will continue until morale improves."

The Beatings Continue

Even with all of the things that can go wrong, pain is the motivator of choice. Most corporations do this. All governments use pain. In fact, our entire legal system is based on the use of pain to motivate right behavior.

The government says, "Don't commit these acts. If you do, we will punish you." The punishment or pain comes in the form of monetary penalties, incarceration, or death.

The government also says, "You must do this. If you fail to do so, we will inflict pain on you." A simple example of this is our body of tax laws that requires everyone to file every year. The laws clearly say, "File and pay your taxes, or else we will punish you."

In one way or another, businesses relay the message, "We want you to increase productivity and improve quality. If you don't, we will reduce your pay, demote you, or even fire you."

An extreme but true example of this was related to me by a friend. He works as a minister in a Las Vegas chapel and conducts ten-minute weddings. The company he works for owns numerous chapels, and the owner uses pain to motivate the company's employees. The owner threatens and quickly fires anyone who even appears to be a problem. In the past year, that owner has fired and replaced 168 people in order to maintain a staff of 38 people. Needless to say, people are not motivated to do anything other than "keep a low profile, don't make waves, and avoid being seen."

Are You a Pain Motivator?

The following test will reveal whether your motivational style makes people want to lash out or leave:

- Do people seem uncomfortable being around you?
- Do people avoid telling you about problem situations?
- Do people make a lot of excuses and blame others for their lack of performance?
- Do you find yourself lecturing or being verbally abusive?
- Is there a lot of tardiness or absenteeism?
- Do people try to avoid you when they see you coming their way?

If you are using pain as your exclusive motivator, you should re-evaluate your true purpose. You are really trying to energize and motivate people to do their best. You are attempting to help people perform at new productivity levels. *Unfortunately, using pain to motivate people backfires in the long run and accomplishes the exact opposite.* Pain may temporarily make people appear more productive, but as soon as the supervisor or manager is not around or has his or her back turned, productivity will decrease.

Motivation is the *willingness* to do work. You cannot verbally or physically beat people into wanting to do a good job. Employing pain usually prevents people from operating at their best.

Motivating with Pleasure

Pleasure also motivates. When people are promised some form of pleasure for being "there," they can be enticed to go "there." Unfortunately, this form of motivation does not work as effectively as it used to. People are more sophisticated and, in many ways, more spoiled. Unless the pleasure offered for being "there" is significant, they may not be motivated to take any real action. The following is an example of how it now takes more pleasure to motivate people to change.

Back in the 1970s, I had reservations on a flight from Japan to Hawaii. The flight was overbooked. A representative of the airlines asked for two volunteers to take a later flight. The volunteers were offered a free, round-trip ticket from the airlines. Almost a dozen people, including me, quickly jumped up to volunteer. The lucky two who were picked were closer to the door than I was.

In another scenario in 1994 I was flying out of Chicago and the flight was overbooked. A representative of the airlines asked whether anyone would be willing to take a later flight for a free, round-trip ticket anywhere the airline flew. No one came forward. I was headed for a speaking engagement and could not afford to take the time. Everyone else must have been busy, because no one volunteered.

Then the representative upped the ante — she offered a round-trip ticket plus two hundred dollars. Still no response. The representative boosted the reward to a round-trip ticket and four hundred dollars! Finally a young man, probably a student, reluctantly stood up and took their offer. These days, it seems that time is a lot more important than money. It takes a lot more pleasure today to motivate people to make a change.

Also, pleasure motivators do not motivate people equally. People are motivated relative to their backgrounds and needs. To a traditional Eskimo living near the Arctic Circle in winter, a bowl of warm whale blubber may be a welcome motivator. To a health conscious person, on the other hand, the mere thought of consuming whale blubber might cause illness. In the same manner, no sane person would dole out his or her last thousand dollars for a gallon of water. But suppose you plunk down that same person in a desert without any water. After a few hours in the sun without water, he or she will gladly part with any amount of money. When their need is great enough, people can be motivated by anything that promises to fulfill that need.

Motivating with pleasure requires that you understand what people need or are lacking in their lives, and then fulfill their needs when they arrive "there."

Identifying Pleasure Motivators

What excites people is the possibility of receiving what they lack. Their needs can be grouped as follows: money, security, appreciation, recognition, and achievement. When you discover what people need, you can elicit better performance by promising to provide what they need after they arrive "there."

For instance, someone who is in need of money is always motivated by the prospect of receiving a monetary bonus. On the other hand, a wealthy person is not motivated by more money, unless it happens to be a lot of money.

To discover what people need, spend some time talking to them. Keep a list of things and events that seem to excite them. When you have discovered their needs, look for unique ways of fulfilling them. These are their motivators. You can energize people by promising to fulfill their needs when they arrive "there."

There are two kinds of motivators: extrinsic and intrinsic. Extrinsic motivators are physical things, such as money, trips, or meals. Intrinsic motivators include expressions of appreciation, recognition, and awards. According to psychologist B. F. Skinner, the way motivation is accomplished is more important than the amount. The following is a list of possible pleasure motivators:

- Tickets to a ball game, concert, or play
- Dinner for two at a favorite restaurant
- A vacation to Hawaii or Las Vegas
- A Caribbean cruise
- A monetary bonus
- A pay raise
- Greater job security
- Acceptance by peers

- Expression of appreciation
- Membership in a high-achievement group with special privileges
- An award for superior performance
- A promotion to a more responsible position
- More independence or autonomy

Often the simplest motivators prove to be the most effective. During my speeches, I often ask to see the hands of those who are recognized and appreciated for their accomplishments every single day. Out of thousands of people, less than a hundred have raised their hands. I then ask if there is anyone who has been showered with such abundant recognition and appreciation that if it happened again tomorrow, it would make them sick. I have never had a single hand go up!

You have heard this before — positive reinforcement. Everyone wants and needs to be recognized and appreciated. They also want to be respected. When they are, they begin to take pride in their work. So try to appreciate people for everything they do, even seemingly ordinary things. You must search for outstanding performance and recognize it. If you do this, the word gets around. Wanting appreciation and recognition themselves, other people will begin to improve their performance.

This works for even the most difficult cases. An example of this is Joe. One day Joe was assigned to my department. He was to retire in less than five months and had a reputation as being a difficult person to work with. He was about as unmotivated as anyone I had ever met. The first time I discussed some of my project concerns with him, he simply took off his glasses, pulled down on one of his lower eyelids, and said, "Do you see anyone in here who gives a damn?"

Now this would have made most managers upset! Instead of becoming angry or frustrated, I took it as a personal challenge. I explained to Joe that when someone retires I usually write that person a great commendation letter, which is read out loud during the company's retirement ceremony. I handed him copies of letters I had written for a couple of others who had just retired.

He looked the letters over and nodded silently. From that moment, Joe was a different person. Anything I wanted, he did. We got along just fine for the five months he had left. Obviously, recognition was an unfulfilled need with Joe. I wrote him a fantastic commendation letter.

You can motivate people without having to write a formal letter. For example, you can do it by writing a complimentary memo when someone does well, giving the original to the person, placing a copy in his or her personnel folder, and tacking a copy on the bulletin board. This motivates the person, increases his or her promotion potential, and has the extra benefit of being an incentive to others. Expressing recognition and genuine appreciation for anything done well goes a long way.

It is also possible to motivate people by providing a special recognition for high achievement. The "Million Dollar Roundtable" is such a recognition. A British client of mine has established an inner circle of the company's highest sales performers. This elite group of "maroon jackets" includes only the best salespeople, who have proven themselves over a period of twenty-five years. The possibility of inclusion in a special group motivates this company's people to meet and exceed the performance requirements.

Reducing the Price of Change

You can also motivate people by becoming a facilitator and helping them to achieve the goals you have set for them. Constantly remind yourself that you are trying to help people to be their best. The following are a few motivators for reducing the price people have to pay to accomplish their goals.

- Provide the right tools and equipment.
- Provide the right training.
- Act as a buffer between your people and the outside world.
- Be open to suggestions for simplifying jobs.
- Reward even small achievements regularly.
- Create and maintain a positive state of being (see Chapter 13).

Effective Motivation

The best form of motivation is a carefully selected combination of both pain and pleasure. You can use a little bit of pain to push people out of "here." At the same time you can offer some form of pleasure to help move them in the right direction to "there."

I used this technique on Bob, one of my young, gung-ho engineers. After a couple of years of outstanding work, Bob had placed his work performance on "cruise control" in a slow downward spiral. He had become engrossed in his personal interests, and his performance was beginning to slip.

To stop this downward trend quickly, I called him into my office and said to him, "Bob, I know that you have a lot of things on your mind. I've been noticing that your performance is not what it used to be. You were someone I could always rely on to come through for us, especially when things got tough."

He was about to say something when I cut him off and continued. "We have a heavy workload over the next couple of months. Right now, I need everyone pulling for us. I really need your total effort. Can I count on you?"

Suddenly, Bob's eyes seemed to get their old spark back again. He said, "Yeah, I guess you know I've been getting involved in a lot of things lately. But you can count on me."

That was all the assurance I needed. Over the next few months, I kept tabs on Bob and he really applied himself. Bob came through when I needed him. I rewarded him by simply taking him out to lunch and writing a complimentary memo to him.

Once in a great while, you may encounter someone who refuses to respond to your suggestions and motivational attempts. When faced with this problem, you must push such people along with a stronger pain motivator. If they still refuse to respond positively, it may then be time to allow them to use their skills somewhere else, perhaps even at your competitor's facility.

Long-term Motivation

It is almost impossible for you to create long-term motivation in other people. Long-term motivation is possible only when they take responsibility for their own careers and lives and motivate themselves. They can accomplish this by applying the techniques found in Chapter 4. You can help them to energize their lives by demonstrating your enthusiasm.

Step 5
Innovate
(ability)

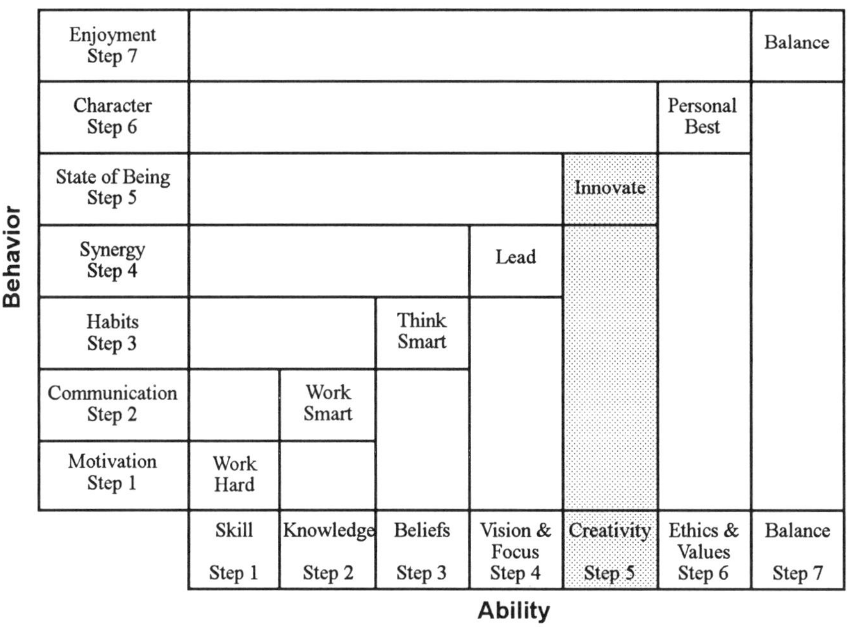

Chapter 12
Step 4: Innovate (ability)
Creativity: Shifting the Paradigm

Every act of creation is first of all an act of destruction.
— Michael Ray and Rochelle Meyers

In a rapidly changing environment, everything quickly becomes obsolete or passé. Some of your competitors will inevitably copy your products and services. A few of your competitors may be developing new products and services that will leapfrog yours. To excel in a highly competitive and rapidly changing environment requires constant improvement of your products or services. Real improvements are realized through the development of creative solutions and ideas to upgrade or transform what you provide to your customers. Without constant improvement, the competition quickly moves in and steals your marketshare.

Unfortunately, too many companies are sitting back, waiting to see how their competitors are doing. Only after a new idea has proven itself do these "wait and see" organizations take any action. You can recognize these companies by the way they characteristically respond to a new idea. They always seem to ask, "Who else is doing it?" However, in a rapidly changing environment, sitting back and waiting can be fatal.

There is a huge profit potential for those companies willing to venture into something unique, something whose time has arrived. Creative improvements can be focused in three directions:

1. Constant improvement of an existing product. Apply innovative ideas to increase the value of products and/or services by improving price, quality or customer service.
2. Developing a new or different use for the existing product. An example of this is the use of brightly colored fishing tackle boxes for storing cosmetics.
3. Creating a completely new product or service, something customers did not know they wanted until it became available. Examples of these items are Post-It Notes, Velcro, and ballpoint pens.

Unfortunately, many companies view creative efforts with reservation. This is understandable because creativity is a resource-consuming activity that may or may not generate any revenue. However, although the risks are high, the rewards can also be great.

Innovation, on the other hand, is relatively safe. Innovation is the steady process of moving the standard another notch higher. The Japanese have a word for the process of continuous improvement. They call it *kaizen.* In practicing kaizen, they are not searching for any paradigm-shifting ideas, although they will use one if it pops up. Instead, they study every single item, every single system, every single process, trying to improve it just a little bit.

Imagine the number of improvements that could be realized if everyone in your organization looked for ways to create them. What price improvements could you realize if everyone searched for ways to reduce costs? What improvements in quality would result if every person concentrated on ideas to create a better product or service? And what fantastic customer service could the organization provide if everyone made regular improvements?

You already possess the talent and ability to become more innovative and creative. You can slip beyond your current mindset and unleash your creative potential. However, creativity is not found through the process commonly referred to as "creative thinking."

All forms of thinking, creative or otherwise, actually restrict you from going beyond your present paradigms. In fact, there is no such thing as creative thinking. The key is in the word "thinking." All thinking is old and static. *True creativity and innovation come from the ability to go beyond thinking.* As Albert Einstein said, "Problems cannot be solved on the same level of mind that created them." Before you try to go beyond thinking, however, you must understand the process of thinking.

Thinking

Thinking is a simple and repetitive process. In thinking, the mind uses three basic functions. These are logic, reason, and memory. When you understand the interaction among these three, you will become aware of how you think. Only then will you be ready to leave the limits of thinking behind and shift into creativity.

Logic

The first basic tool in thinking is the function of logic. As you may have learned in basic philosophy, logic is the application of the rules of thinking. Ten basic rules completely define how you and I think. Here, we will touch upon two.

If you are a logical thinker, you must follow these rules. No deviation is allowed. If your thinking fails to follow these rules, it will be called "illogical." An example of one of these rules goes like this:

If A, then B.
A, therefore B.

In a real-life example, it would read, "If it rains, then we will not have a picnic. It's raining, therefore we will not have a picnic." You accept this as a perfectly logical statement.

If the statement were changed so that it read differently, you would not accept it as being logical. If someone said, "If it rains, then we will not have a picnic. It is raining, therefore we will have the picnic," you would immediately reject the statement. You would criticize the person who made that statement as an illogical person.

Here is another rule of logic:

If A = C and B = C,
Then A = B.

An example of this would be, "If Mary is twenty-five years of age, and John is twenty-five years of age, then Mary and John are the same age."

Logic is the application of ten rules, over and over again. As long as you follow these ten rules to the letter, you are regarded as a logical thinker. There is nothing creative or intuitive about logic.

Reason

Reason is the second tool of thinking and limits what a person will accept. If a statement approaches those limits, a reasonable person will begin to question the validity of the statement. If a statement goes beyond those limits, he or she will almost automatically reject that statement.

People have established reasonable limits, whether they know it or not, on almost everything in their lives. They reject any statements or conclusions that go beyond what they consider "reasonable," even when they prove to be completely logical. The following is an example I sometimes use in my presentations.

I ask one of the participants, "Suppose you were really, really thirsty. How long would it take you to drink a glass of water?" The usual answer is "about thirty seconds."

I then tell the person, "Logic says that if you can drink a glass of water in about thirty seconds, you can drink two glasses in one minute." The audience usually "gets" where I am going with this point and begins to laugh.

I continue with, "Following the rules of logic, I conclude that you can drink 120 glasses of water in an hour and 240 in two hours."

This is where your reason kicks in. Even though this statement is perfectly logical, you know this is not possible. You may recall how difficult a time you have drinking even eight glasses of water in a day. You intuitively "know" that drinking 120 glasses of water in an hour is absolutely impossible.

Reason is a valuable tool for identifying what goes beyond acceptable limits. It rejects things that are beyond what your experience or imagined experience will accept. When you do this automatically, as most people have been doing for most of their lives, you become stuck with your paradigms. Your need to set "reasonable" limits often rejects both creative and innovative ideas.

Most people's reasoning would have rejected the idea of joining the ends of a plastic hose, and then selling it as a toy. Reason would have laughed at the idea of selling ordinary rocks as pets. Even the idea of using a lousy glue that hardly works on a piece of paper would have been thrown out — but this is the idea that generated the Post It Notes.

My wife's grandfather is an example of reason rejecting a creative idea. Many years ago, he had an opportunity to invest in a patent for a glass prism. This prism took light in and reflected it back to its source. His mental "reason" told him that no one would buy this idea. After all, a mirror does a better job. However, what he turned down was the universal principle on which all reflectors, such as those in the taillights of all automobiles, is based.

To tap your creative level of mind, you have to be willing to put aside your reasonable limits for the moment. For the moment, entertain ideas that a "reasonable" person would never consider or would reject as being unreasonable. You have to leave the safety net of "who else is doing it" behind. You must be willing to take a risk to be the first.

Memory

The final tool of thinking is the ability to recall information previously gathered. People can remember only the information they have already collected. If they did not obtain a specific bit of information earlier, it is impossible to recall it.

Through the function of your memory, you can recall your name and birthday. You can remember complex ideas and formulas. What you cannot recall is something that was never in there in the first place, such as my middle name.

Thus the whole process of thinking is stored in your memory. The logical formulas you use, the "reasonable" limits you have, and the data you use are all stored in your memory. Creative and innovative ideas are *not stored* there. Unique ideas cannot be found in your memory because they are, by definition, new and unknown to you.

Beyond Paradigms

With only logic, reason, and memory to work with, thinking can be likened to a computer. You simply get out of it whatever was put into it. *To go beyond memory into creativity and innovation, you must be willing to leave logic, reason, and memory behind.*

I know that this may sound scary to a few of you. After all, you have only known logic, reason, and memory. *But if you are willing, you can deliberately go beyond the limits of your paradigms into endless possibilities.*

Tapping the creative mind begins by exhausting all possibilities available through your normal thinking process consisting of logic, reason, and memory. You must consider these options first; otherwise your mind will tend to rush back to the process of thinking.

When you have exhausted the possibilities thinking can create, you can begin to practice various procedures to tap the creative part of your mind, your subconscious mind. After you obtain an insight, you can bring it into form.

A systematic strategy for tapping your creative mind requires the following steps:

1. Identify the purpose.
2. Select a group.
3. Create a supportive culture.
4. Brainstorm for solutions.
5. Ask dumb questions.
6. Program the subconscious mind.
7. Wait for a creative insight.
8. Bring the idea into form.

Identifying the Purpose

Most people have a warped view of creative people. They envision eccentric, unusually dressed folks who stare into space and wait for a light bulb to flash over their heads. It flashes, they jump up, and out spews an unusual piece of art or perhaps a new book.

This form of creativity can sometimes work in the artistic world, but in the business world, a much more practical approach is required. For creativity to be useful, you must focus your effort on improving a particular product or service. You can begin by identifying what you are going to improve. Are you trying to build a better coffee machine, streamline a massage service you offer, or build a new type of airplane? To identify your purpose, ask yourself some questions that clarify what you are trying to accomplish.

Innovative Improvement of an Existing Product or Service

You can begin by identifying which of your existing products or services you are going to improve. To help you focus your energies, answer the following questions:

1. Which of the three value factors are we trying to improve?

   Are we trying to reduce the price?

   Are we trying to improve quality?

   Are we attempting to improve the service we provide?

2. Why do we want to do this?

   Is our overall value noncompetitive?

   Is our price too high?

   Is poor quality so apparent that customers are not buying?

   Is poor quality resulting in too many service calls or returns?

   Is our service capacity inadequate to meet service demands?

3. What is the competition doing?

   What is the present industry standard?

   What does the competition do better than we do?

   What do we do better than the competition does?

   Does the competition have a technical advantage over us?

   How can we regain or maintain a technical advantage?

   Does the competition have a cost advantage over us?

   How can we reduce our costs?

4. Who are our customers?

   What real benefits do they realize with our products or services?

   What feature is most important to our customers?

Do people use our products for reasons other than the one we intended?

Can we adapt our product or service to meet people's other needs?

Can a handicapped person benefit from our product or service?

5. Have our customers changed?

What is the demographic breakdown?

How has it changed over the past year?

Have our customers' expectations risen?

What is their primary focus when they buy?

6. What strategic advantages are available?

Do we or do our competitors have a location advantage?

Do we or do our competitors have a tax advantage?

Do we or do our competitors have an information access advantage?

Do we or do our competitors have a talent advantage?

Do we or do our competitors have a superior culture?

How can we match or *surpass* their advantage?

7. How can we do this cheaper, faster, or easier?

What is the easiest way we can do this?

What is the fastest way we can do this?

Is this new technique or process sustainable?

What technology will make the *entire* process cheaper or faster?

By answering the questions above, you can identify where to direct your innovative efforts.

Creative Development of a New Product or Service

To develop a new product or service, you must identify what customers are willing to purchase. Customers want products and services that either simplify their tasks or make them look or feel better.

To identify what people would like to purchase, ask the following questions:

1. What could we provide that customers would love to have, if it were possible?

   What new product or service would the customer love to have or use?

   What benefit does it really give the customer?

2. What problems or fears do people face?

   Are they willing to solve these problems for a price?

   Is the number of sufferers large enough?

   Are the problems recurring?

   Are we qualified to solve the problems?

   Is expertise available to solve the problems?

3. What desires do people have?

   Are there enough people with a particular desire?

   What are people willing to pay to fulfill their desires?

   Can we educate people to have a specific desire?

   Are we in the right position to fulfill their desires?

   Can we fulfill their desires profitably?

Selecting the Group

In most cases, artistic creativity and innovation are best done by one person. But in our increasingly complex business environment, creativity and innovation are most effectively achieved in a group or team setting.

Members of the group should come from all disciplines that will contribute to the final product or service. Members may include representatives from engineering, marketing, sales, manufacturing, service personnel, and human resources.

When selecting the members of the group, ask for volunteers. People who are forced to participate are rarely very creative. From the volunteers, select the special few who are excited by the proposed project.

Keep the number of participants limited. Six to eight people is ideal. I would not recommend more than ten. Larger groups become unwieldy and difficult to work with.

Cultural diversity is a powerful asset you are when trying to discover a creative or innovative solution. In a homogeneous culture, people all think in a similar fashion. As illustrated in the figure below, people with similar backgrounds and training all look at the problem from similar points of view. They all see the same obstacle. They will probably suggest similar solutions for overcoming that obstacle.

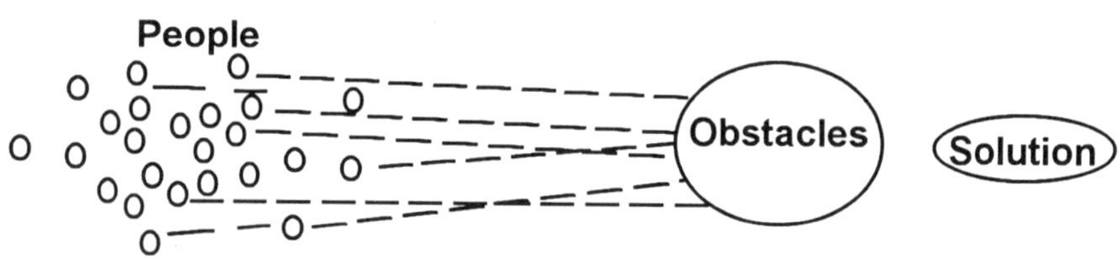

Figure 12-1: Individual Viewpoints without Cultural Diversity

This is one reason that most Japanese have a problem with creative ideas. They are an example of a very homogeneous culture. They have been trained to think in a similar manner. In their culture, diversity is frowned upon. Essentially, "the nail that stands out is hammered down."

In a diverse culture, people have different backgrounds and training. They may analyze the situation uniquely and process the information differently. Seeing the problem from a different point of view, they may then approach the solution from a novel angle. As shown in the figure on the opposite page, together, they have a better chance of discovering a workable solution around the obstacle or issue.

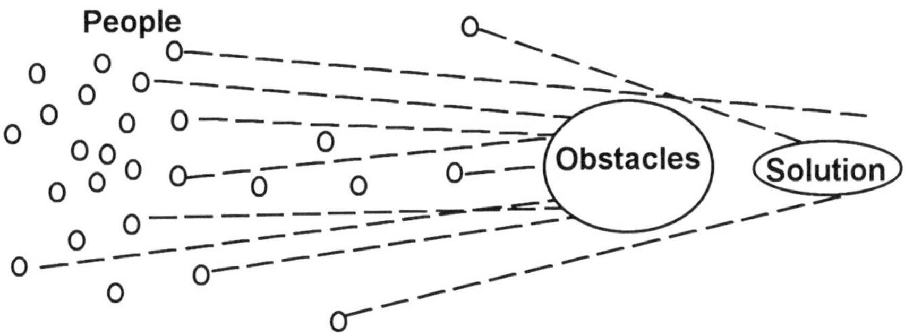

Figure 12-2: Individual Viewpoints with Cultural Diversity

To stimulate creativity, I encourage you to embrace diversity. Welcome those who have different values and beliefs. Only in a diverse group will you be able to tap their differences and make the diversity a valuable tool for discovering solutions.

Creating a Supportive Culture

After you have the right group or team, you have to create a supportive environment. A supportive environment is one in which each member feels comfortable making suggestions and exchanging ideas. A supportive culture has the following attributes:

1. A safe feeling: You need a culture in which people feel that it is safe to propose ideas, even wild and strange ideas. The primary stumbling block to creativity and innovation is fear. The fear of failure and the fear of looking foolish stop people from making suggestions. Fear of negative feedback from colleagues may prevent some members from saying anything really unusual.

2. Freedom from distractions: You need an environment in which people are free from constant routine distractions. Creativity cannot blossom in the middle of distractions. Committee meetings, deadlines, and phone calls limit or dash the creative spark. Paperwork, repetitive analysis, delays, and lack of follow-up action destroy creativity. You must find a way to isolate the group, at least temporarily.

3. Empowerment to take action: You must allow people the freedom to offer suggestions and then to explore creative solutions. When everyone is allowed to participate freely, they can claim ownership of the results. They will then be willing to go the extra mile to make the team's ideas work.
4. The right mental state: Creativity flourishes when you have a positive state of being. A positive attitude, emotional control, and strong self-esteem go a long way to support your creative efforts. Developing and maintaining the right state of being is covered in the following chapters.
5. Humility: You must realize that no one has all of the right answers or the only answer. Your suggestions, as well as those of everyone else, should be accepted as possibilities.
6. A sense of wonder and play: Remember that children are most creative when they are playing. They allow their imagination to wander everywhere and generate many new ideas. You must try to recapture that sense of play and fun that you once had as a child. When you are really enjoying yourself, your imagination can flow.

What Not To Do

I once worked as a civil servant for the United States government. To reduce costs and increase productivity, the government had established an incentive program for new ideas. It promised to pay employees 10 percent of all verifiable cost savings over a period of three years.

Along with two other engineers and a technician, I got right to work. We had an idea that could potentially save thousands of dollars. When we finally finished, we submitted the idea to the GAO (General Accounting Office). The GAO estimated cost savings over the next three years of three million dollars.

It did not take a genius to calculate that 10 percent of three million dollars was 300 thousand dollars. One-fourth of that was seventy-five thousand dollars. In those days, that was many times larger than my annual salary. We were understandably excited. We were bursting with many more ideas to submit, many of which we had known about for a long time.

Our entire organization gathered for the award ceremony. It was then announced that the award had been reduced from 300 thousand dollars to a miniscule total of one thousand dollars.

I thought to myself, "Well, 250 dollars is better than nothing."

Then the names were called for recognition. The other two engineers were called. To make a long story short, eight other people, including my supervisor, were called. The technician and I were never called.

I was totally disheartened. After the ceremony, my supervisor approached the technician and me. He wanted to sign his check over to us. I refused to accept it. We stopped all work on our other ideas.

The cost reduction program died that day. In a few days, people from around the world were calling to ask whether our awards had really been reduced. When I verified what they had heard, their cost-saving ideas also went dormant.

Although it is sometimes difficult to establish and maintain a creative and supportive culture, you must. You can accelerate your career if you can discover tomorrow's innovative new products and services.

Brainstorming for Solutions

When you have established a creative environment, you are ready to create a brainstorm. Begin by selecting one area and asking people for ideas or possible solutions. When brainstorming for solutions, you need a storm. A storm can grow only if the first clouds in the sky are not immediately deflated.

In other words, *all* ideas must be accepted. No one should be allowed to criticize or say anything negative about any idea. Albert Einstein said, "Imagination is more important than knowledge." No matter how foolish or impossible an idea may sound, it must be accepted.

One simple yet enjoyable way to reinforce this idea is to issue everyone a water pistol. As soon as someone criticizes or downplays an idea, that person can be "shot" or squirted by everyone else.

As ideas are being generated, have someone record everyone's ideas on three-by-five-inch cards. Tape each card to the wall, grouping common ideas into categories, such as new service ideas, faster service, better service methods, and so on. Keep reminding people that all ideas are good ideas, no matter how impractical or impossible they may sound. Every idea, even if it is impossible to implement or use, may be the springboard or seed for another idea that may work.

Keep recording until the group has temporarily exhausted all ideas. With these ideas before the group, select one area and have everyone concentrate on it, using the following techniques:

1. Expand on an idea.
2. Use free association to transfer ideas.
3. Twist reality.

Expand on an Idea

Focus on one area and ask everyone for ideas and comments on that area. If someone identifies a problem with an idea, first acknowledge and record it, then refocus people on finding workable solutions. If the group is allowed to concentrate on the problem, the session can easily become a nonproductive gripe session.

Again record every new idea or solution on a three-by-five inch card, and post it on the wall. Then have everyone build on each idea that is posted by asking the following questions:

- Can this basic concept do something else? The perfume atomizer was the basis for the automobile carburetor.
- Can two or more of these ideas be combined to create something else? Weak glue and a place holder in a song book created the Post-It Note.
- Do any of these ideas trigger other ideas? Burrs on socks triggered the development of Velcro.

Use Free Association to Transfer Ideas

To obtain more ideas, use free association. Use something totally unrelated to the subject to see whether it will trigger any new ideas. The following are some examples:

- Pick a book at random, open it to any page, and read it out loud.
- Play with children's blocks of different shapes and colors.

- Close your eyes and touch various objects (shapes).
- Draw with your left hand. Use your right hand if you are left-handed.
- Take a walk and use whatever you see to trigger ideas.
- Choose a picture (photo) book. Open to any page and study the picture.
- Listen to unusual music.
- Move to a different seat in the room.

Record any new ideas that come to mind. Do not be discouraged if you are having some problems. You are still only tapping the surface of your creative mind.

Twist Reality

Twisting reality is another tool for triggering creative solutions. Have someone in the group ask any of the following "What if . . ." questions:

- "What if the rules were different?"
- "What if we could not fail?"
- "What if we had unlimited resources?"
- "What if we could overcome the impossible?"
- "What if (fill in the blank) were not true?"

Record any ideas that may become possible. Remember, this is not serious. You are operating within the context of your mental playground. Let it be free! Allow it to play with some totally outrageous solutions. Entertain solutions that are crazy, totally out in left field. Again, in developing creative or innovative ideas and solutions, no one knows what crazy idea will lead to something outstanding.

Asking Dumb Questions

The group's ideas now need to be shared with others. It is time to allow co-workers who are not members of the group a chance to comment on your ideas. Set down the following ground rules: As people offer their ideas and comments, no one in the core group is permitted to become defensive. If nonmembers feel any resentment coming from the core group, they may simply stop commenting. Remember to keep it light. This is play, and the group is trying to have some fun. Be especially aware of useful comments such as,

"Why are you doing this? It would have been so much better and easier if you . . ."

"This is great, but you should . . ."

"I just saw this new thing that will . . ."

Record comments as they are made. Remember, you are searching for new ideas. Even really outrageous ideas should be recorded. At the same time, each member of the group should listen attentively and record any new ideas that come to mind.

Now have someone ask some *really* dumb questions. If possible, ask the core group's friends and family members to comment on the group's ideas. Be acutely aware as they ask questions such as,

"What are you really trying to do?"

"Why even do this?"

"Who would want to use this?"

"Do we really need this?"

"Wouldn't it be easier if . . ."

"Wouldn't it be better if . . ."

"So what?"

These questions and statements might shock you, but they are very important. They are coming from a totally different point of view. Sometimes those who are closest to an idea have the most difficulty in seeing an obvious, different, or unusual possibility.

At this point, you have probably exhausted everything you and the rest of the group can possibly think of. You are now ready to go beyond thinking. Remember, exhausting all possibilities is important. If you fail to do this, your thinking process will automatically search for answers through logic, reason, and memory. Only after it has tried everything will it be ready to go beyond thinking into the subconscious or creative mind.

Programming the Subconscious Mind

Your subconscious mind is the door through which you obtain new ideas, solutions, and insights. You can open this door by mentally programming yourself to do so.

Say the following programming statement to yourself. Say it out loud, with strong feeling. Your feelings are the key that allows a programming statement to enter deep into your subconscious mind.

Programming Yourself to Solve a Specific Problem

I am in need of a solution for ____________ (problem you need to solve).

The real nature of my problem is ____________.

What I wish to achieve is ____________.

(greater productivity/efficiency, lower cost, more capability, new marketing approach, new markets, new method, better look, improved interaction, better service, new product, higher quality, wider appeal, new service, and so on.)

I really want creative (or innovative) solutions.

I know that creative (or innovative) solutions are already coming, NOW!

I am prepared to receive, record, consider, and use the appropriate solutions.

When you have completed programming your mind, wait for a solution. Because the solution may come at any time, have a pen and paper handy, both day and night. How long should you wait? As long as it takes.

Waiting for a Creative Insight

Creative insights come in many different formats. They usually come when your thinking mind becomes silent. The following are a few possible moments when there is a greater probability you will receive an intuitive flash:

1. Dreaming. Your dreams can contain a wealth of creative ideas. Dream solutions have been used by Edison, Mozart, Einstein, Robert Louis Stevenson, and Eli Whitney, to name a few. If you program your mind just before going to sleep, you have a greater chance of having a creative insight. Have a pen and paper next to your bed to record what you receive.

I have found that dreams are one of the most powerful tools for solving problems or gaining a creative insight. I have used them during most of my career. When I give speeches or lectures on dreams, I find that approximately 60 percent of my audience have used their dreams to solve business and personal problems. This is such a useful tool that I wrote a book on dreams, *Creative Dream Analysis: A Guide to Self-Development.*

2. Just after waking. In the quiet moments just after waking, you have the opportunity to tap your creative mind. As you lay quietly with your eyes closed, ask for a creative or innovative solution to the problem. Then wait. Alternatively, you can play the "what if . . ." scenario. Often, in a flash, an idea may come to you. Record whatever comes.
3. Daydreaming. An idea may come to you while you are staring out the window, relaxing in the bathtub, or looking at a wall. A new approach or solution may occur whenever your thoughts become silent.
4. Meditating. During meditation, you may tap into the creative alpha level of mind and receive a creative insight. Meditation is simply the process of silencing your thoughts for a period of time.
5. Performing a repetitive task. While you are performing a "no-brainer" physical activity, an idea may occur to you. Walking, swimming, and gardening are great ways to tap your creativity.
6. Enjoying a view. A unique approach or solution may occur while you are watching a sunset, or listening to a waterfall or to the wind blowing through the trees. All of these can quiet your thinking mind and allow an inspirational moment.

You can never predict when creative ideas will occur. Arthur Jones envisioned seashells during a bout of insomnia and created the Nautilus machine. Mitsuro Ida, designer of the Walkman, finds the bathroom his favorite place to envision new ideas. Creative ideas can come to life in the most unexpected places.

Whenever you receive a creative insight, you must record the idea immediately. Creative ideas can fade as quickly as your dreams fade in the morning. Like your dreams, creative ideas occur at a different level of mind, which is outside thinking and memory. As such, they are often difficult to remember.

Also, there may be occasions when you cannot immediately record these creative insights. If this should happen, repeat the idea over and over to yourself until you have a chance to write it down. If you stop repeating it for even a little while, you may lose it. You can minimize this problem by always being prepared to record your creative solutions and approaches.

Bringing an Idea into Form

It is now time to develop your ideas into a useful product or service. This is where most people fail. Most good ideas die with the inventor. To accelerate your career, you have to bring ideas into reality.

This is also where a lot of companies fail. They develop a great product or service, then fail to refine it, bring it to market, and capitalize on it.

The Swiss created the quartz movement, but Texas Instruments and Seiko brought it to market. The Japanese invented the first television set in 1926, but it was developed by the Americans. Currently, television manufacturing is done primarily in Japan. Ampex created the first Video Tape Machine, which was mass-marketed by the Japanese. The Germans created the internal combustion engine, but the Americans brought it to market on a mass production basis.

Bringing an idea into marketable form usually requires tremendous dedication and financial backing. This is where many individuals and organizations give up. Sony produced the Walkman only because of the dedication and belief of its chairman, Akio Morita. It was Fred Smith's complete belief in his vision of Federal Express that made it real.

Fortunately, innovation does not require that kind of dedication. Innovation is the steady improvement of what already exists. You can evaluate the possibilities and expand the applications into different areas.

Combining a tape recorder that did not record with a headphone created the Walkman. Using the radar magnetron to warm foods was the basis for the microwave oven. Modifying the size of a ballpoint pen and adapting the concept resulted in the underarm deodorant roller. The possibilities are endless.

Step 5
Innovate
(behavior)

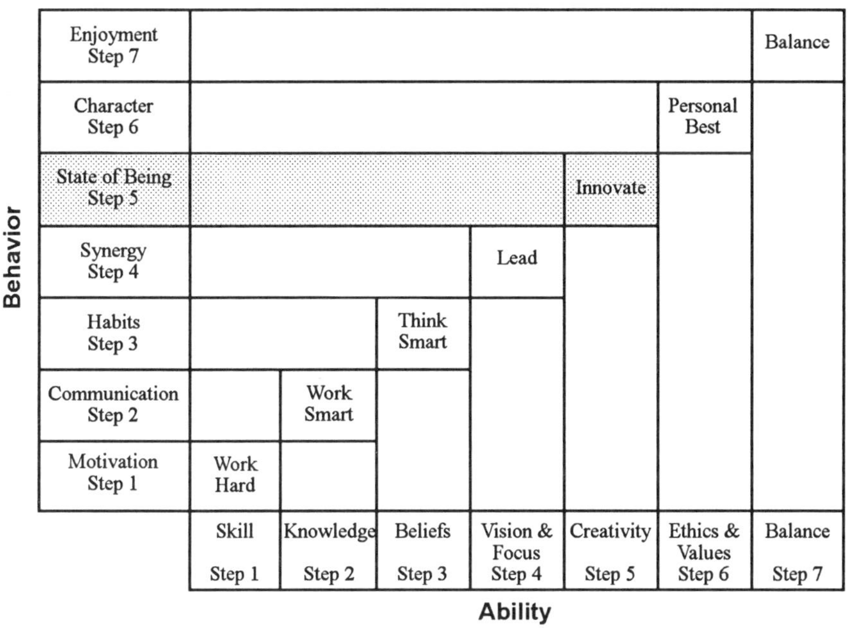

Chapter 13
Step 5: Innovate (behavior)
State of Being

People can make or break a company. Management can do whatever it wants with the banks and borrowing and manipulating and everything else. If the spirit of the people isn't in everything they do, it's going to fail.
— Vic Barouh

State of being is one of the most difficult aspects of individual performance to understand and modify. It is your psychological energy, the enthusiasm you have for life. It is made up of five almost ethereal factors, including your emotions, stress level, attitude, self-image, and self-esteem. The effect of all these factors on your psyche creates your state of being.

Your state of being is the sum total of how you feel. When your state of being decreases, you feel tired and drained. When you feel down, your motivation sags. At the same time, your performance and productivity drop.

Conversely, when your state of being increases, you feel good about life. You feel enthusiastic and ready to move forward. Your energy level remains high, even as you deal with difficult projects and situations. Additionally, your performance level rises to greatly elevated levels.

To attain professional power and personal excellence, you need to maintain a positive state of being. Like most people, you may find that constantly maintaining a positive state of being seems almost impossible. Your state of being seems to decrease for any number of reasons. It might be the result of an IRS audit, a bad meeting with the boss, or simply a bad-hair day. It might have happened when an idiot cut you off on the way to work or during the bad service you got at the restaurant. Whatever the cause, the result is always the same. When your state of being goes down or becomes negative, your performance always suffers.

The secret to operating at optimum levels is to gain and maintain control of your state of being. You cannot let outside circumstances pull you down and lower your performance.

A Negative State of Being

When your state of being becomes negative, your performance drops dramatically. Every part of your life is directly affected by your state of being. Some of the more common results of a negative state of being include the following:

1. Skills are diminished. The quality of your work tends to go down and you tend to make more mistakes. Accidents often happen at this time.

2. Motivation goes down. You tend to feel drained and lose your enthusiasm about everything. Customers, clients, and co-workers see you as unhappy or, worse, not caring.

3. Communication is impaired. You tend to hear the wrong information and/or say the wrong thing.

4. Understanding becomes distorted. You incorrectly process what you experience and reach the wrong conclusion. With the wrong conclusion, you make the wrong decision and take the wrong action.

5. Focusing becomes difficult. You tend to get off track or concern yourself with unimportant things.

6. Working closely with others becomes difficult. You do not like working with others, and they do not like working with you. Customers do not like to build relationships with negative people.

7. Appearance seems immature. Management loses confidence in your ability to handle important issues and critical

situations. You do not transmit the essential aura of success and control. Promotion possibilities pass you by.

8. Influence on others becomes negative. Other people hate to be pulled down to your level and tend to avoid you.

As you can see, a negative state of being ruins your performance. More than that, a negative state of being also reduces the performance of others. This is especially critical in management positions and leadership roles. A negative state of being can lower your bottom-line results and the results of those around you.

A Positive State of Being

On the other hand, a positive state of being greatly improves your performance. It improves your interpersonal relationships with your family, relatives, and co-workers. It also has a positive effect on others and helps them to improve their own state of being.

Fortunately, your state of being is totally under your control. Although outer circumstances and other people appear to alter your state of being, you can control it. *The better you manage your state of being, the greater your ability to direct your future.* You can free yourself from the negative influences of others.

Influencing Others

Your state of being influences the state of being of other people. There is an old saying: "Everyone loves a lover." Why do people love to be in the company of lovers? Because it makes them feel good. In the same manner, you probably love to be in the company of people who are in love or happy. When others are having a good time, it is much easier for you to enjoy yourself.

Some people are able to quickly change the state of being of other people. These people are the most highly paid people in the world. This group includes actors and actresses, musicians, magicians and illusionists, and humorists. They have a talent for changing the audience's state of being almost instantly.

No one goes to a movie, a musical concert, or an amusement park to receive an education. People go to a movie or concert to enjoy themselves. They want to *feel* different. It does not matter what the feeling is. It could be fear from a roller coaster or a scary movie. It could be love from a movie or joy from a symphony concert. Whatever the source, people want to change their state of being.

Why do people want to change their state of being? I believe it is because most people are simply bored. Every workday seems almost identical to every other workday. The weekends seem monotonously similar. This is why people look forward to a vacation. They want to change their monotonous lives through an experience. They want to feel alive!

Your State of Being

Before you can change your state of being, you must determine its level. For the categories listed below, identify the level of your state of being at work, in the evening, and during weekends:

Ecstatic	+3
Happy	+2
Good	+1
Numb	0
Worried	-1
Stressed	-2
Angry/Terrified	-3

Most people can identify where they are on the table above at any given time. This level determines the direction toward which you can draw other people. When you are feeling terrific, you can pull the rest of the people around you to a more positive level. However, the reverse is also true. When you are stressed, angry, or terrified, you tend to drag everyone down toward your level.

As you interact with other people who are at a different state of being, you automatically try to pull them to your level as they try to pull you toward theirs. You can see that there is much truth to the saying, "Everyone creates enlightenment. Some when they enter a room, others when they leave."

All people, even those who are considered "toxic," can be influenced by a positive state of being. To have a positive influence on others, you must maintain your positive state of being despite their negative state of being. In the war of influence, *the person who is most committed to maintaining his or her state of being ultimately influences the other.*

Having and maintaining a positive state of being is a wonderful asset for your career and your personal life. In all interactions with other people, your presence helps others to become more positive. People love to be around those who are positive. They love to do business with people who are positive. A positive state of being will help your career and all of your relationships.

Leadership

A positive state of being is also a powerful leadership tool. With it, you can have a positive influence on your workers' state of being. They, in turn, can have a powerful influence on your customers.

Unfortunately, you cannot order others to have a positive state of being. Many leaders are ignorant of this fact and make statements such as the following:

"When you're here, just remember to smile and have a positive attitude."

"Just act happy and give great service."

"Don't bring your personal problems to work! Leave them at home."

Ordering people to be positive or happy never makes it so. They may do as they were told, smiling and acting as if everything were fine. But deep down inside, they become even more upset and even resentful. Their performance suffers and everyone around them, including customers, can feel their negative state of being.

Leadership is not the process of ordering people around. *Leadership is the art of guiding and demonstrating what you want people to become.* If you want positive people, you must first attain and maintain a positive state of being. Only when you can consistently demonstrate a positive state of being can you influence others to change.

The influencing power of a positive state of being on others was well known to the "shoguns," the Japanese warlords. During a battle, a shogun positioned himself on a hilltop overlooking the battlefield. There he sat, gave orders to his men, and provided a psychological anchor.

Whenever things got tough for his troops, they quickly glanced back to the top of the hill. If the shogun was still there, unmoved, looking totally confident and committed to winning, they knew that their side was still doing well. Their state of being rose accordingly and they doubled their efforts in the battle.

However, if they turned and saw the shogun taking up his sword to defend himself or getting ready to leave, they knew that things were not going their way. Their state of being began to falter. It was only a matter of time before they lost heart, turned, and ran.

In the same manner, leading and influencing others requires that you maintain a positive state of being yourself. How committed would you be if the managers and executives in your organization seemed bothered by business events and you saw them submitting their resumes to other companies? You would probably update your own resume as soon as you could and begin looking for another job, too.

The people with whom you interact are very aware of your state of being. When your state of being is positive, others feel more positive about themselves. They are more open and receptive to your ideas and the changes you propose.

If your state of being becomes negative, they will sense it immediately. People tend not to "buy" into your ideas when they sense negativity. They become suspicious, wondering where you are really coming from. They may simply decide to take a "wait and see" attitude or outright reject what you are saying. No one can lead others while feeling down or while preparing to retreat.

Of course, you can influence others by using a negative state of being. Angry outbursts and threats can make being "here" very painful for others and motivate them into action. However, although they may appear to take action, they also want to leave or take revenge. As the old saying goes, "What goes around, comes around." Using a negative state of being will eventually backfire on you.

Commitment

As I mentioned before, your state of being is truly infectious. The way you feel influences other people, just as the way they feel affects you. In the game of influencing others, commitment is the key. The person who is most committed to his or her state of being wins.

When a child is upset, parents are immediately drawn into a battle of state of being. While the parent wants to make the child's state of being more positive, the child is committed to remaining upset. If the parent becomes upset or angry, the child has won. Parents must maintain their positive state of being in all interactions.

When you are feeling positive and are interacting with someone who has a negative state of being, the battle of commitment begins. If the other person's resolve to remain negative is more powerful than your determination to remain positive, his or her state of being will pull you down. The other person may have "won," but both parties lose.

Therefore it is important that you always maintain a positive state of being. When you stay positive in a group, your state of being causes others to become more positive. As their state of being improves, yours rises, too. The final outcome is an upward or improving spiral. Everything gets better. The upward spiral can be seen clearly at the gaming table when someone is winning. Suddenly everyone at the table is feeling good and others crowd around to feel the energy and excitement. They want their state of being to be pulled into the upward spiral.

Naturally the opposite is also true. When you allow others to pull you down, you then pull them further down. The downward spiral brings everyone down. This can be observed in people who are experiencing a sad event, such as a funeral or a tragic accident.

Your state of being is made up of five components: emotions, stress level, attitude, self-image, and self-esteem. Let us see how you can control your state of being by raising each component and keeping it positive.

Chapter 14
Step 5: Innovate (behavior)
Emotions: Handling Negative Emotions

Temper is what gets most of us into trouble. Pride is what keeps us there.
— Unknown

The first component of state of being, emotions, is a very touchy subject. Although emotions are a part of human nature, there are times when being emotional is a liability. In a business setting or in a personal relationship, becoming negatively emotional often becomes a problem.

Under normal working conditions, you are a logical and rational human being. You usually act appropriately, accumulate the necessary data, evaluate the situation, and weigh the possibilities. Then, based on your logic and sometimes "gut feelings," you make your decisions. All of your problems are solved in this logical and systematic manner.

Having positive emotions does not usually pose a problem. When your emotions are exceptionally positive, they cause you to view the world through rose-colored glasses. You see the world as a nicer place to live. You feel wonderful and this makes all of your interactions appear nicer. At the same time, positive emotions make others feel better about you and themselves. Positive emotions are a wonderful asset.

Negative Emotions

It is when your emotions turn darker that real problems can appear. Negative emotions distort your perception of reality. The world begins to look darker and more negative. You are not able to see situations clearly. Your negative emotions cloud your ability to understand what is really happening and alter the information you receive.

With inputs distorted by negative emotions, you are more likely to perceive situations incorrectly. Based on your incorrect perception, the decisions you make may be skewed in the wrong direction. You may then say and do the wrong things. This can create problems for others and ultimately, for you.

Negative emotions also make everyone uncomfortable. When you become negatively emotional, you tend to make others want to leave. Of course you can later apologize for your behavior. But apologies are often not enough. People remember an emotional outburst long after the incident is over. In their minds, they perceive those who cannot control their emotions as being immature. In the end, you may discover that true forgiveness for an emotional outburst may be impossible to obtain.

My wife and I experienced such a negative emotional incident with a postal worker one day. We were taking the mail to the post office for the 6 p.m. drop, the latest pickup time in our area. Because we often work up to the last minute, we find ourselves rushing there just in time to make the last pickup.

On this particular day, we arrived about two minutes before 6 p.m. There was a new woman postal worker collecting the mail, one we had never seen before. She was rushing back and forth, collecting the mail from multiple mailboxes.

Wanting to make sure her mail was picked up that day, my wife ran up to the woman and said, "I need to make today's mail. Which box haven't you picked up yet?"

The woman glared at my wife and began yelling all kinds of criticisms and a few obscene words.

My wife was completely taken aback. She watched the woman stomping back to another box and realized that the collection was from north to south. The postal worker had not picked up the last two boxes, so my wife quickly ran over and placed her packages there. Meanwhile, other last-minute mailers began arriving and rushed over, asking the same question of the carrier. Each person received the same torrent of incomprehensible, almost violent words.

As we drove away, my wife said, "You know, I think the woman is crazy. Her eyes looked crazed. At least she was crazy when she was yelling at me."

After a pause she continued, "I think I should call and report her. Not to hurt her, but to help her. The woman definitely needs some psychiatric help. What do you think?"

I shrugged my shoulders and replied, "We shouldn't judge the woman so harshly. We don't know what she may be going through today. Maybe someone in her family just died. Maybe she got some bad news about one of her kids. Maybe she's just having a really bad day."

With that, we drove off to have dinner.

The next day found us working late again, trying to finish some things that had to be mailed that day. At a few minutes before 6 p.m., we were about a block from the post office.

I smiled as I turned to my wife and asked, "Won't it be funny if the same woman is collecting the mail again?"

She turned to me and frowned, "That's not funny. I hope she isn't there. I wouldn't want to have to confront her again."

As we drove up to the post office, the mail truck was parked next to the outdoor boxes. I could also see that it was the same postal worker picking up the mail. I chuckled and dragged out a, "Sheeeeee's heeeere."

My wife got out and deliberately walked toward the boxes. As she got closer, the postal worker, who was bent inside the box, looked up and noticed her. She stopped what she was doing and stood up. I could almost feel my wife cringe.

The postal worker smiled a big smile and waved. My wife waved back and then deposited her envelopes.

When my wife got back into the car, she looked at me excitedly and said, "Did you see what she did? Did you see? She smiled and waved at me."

"I know."

Thoughtfully, she observed, "You may have been right. She was probably just having a bad day. I'm glad I didn't report her."

The next day, we again arrived at the post office at 6 p.m. The same postal worker was there again, doing her job. This time my wife took a few minutes to talk to the woman, getting to know her a little bit better. They are now on a first-name basis.

Unlike my wife, some people would not have forgiven the postal worker. They might have written a letter to the postmaster to complain about her behavior. No matter how sweet her future actions became, they might never have seen her as a nice person.

You must never allow negative emotions or anger to rule you in any situation. If you do, you will lose your ability to react quickly. You will find yourself unable to respond intelligently. Your negative emotions will shut down your ability to see clearly. Not seeing clearly immediately limits your ability to think. Even more than that, your negative emotions can make you lose control of your actions.

You must learn to control or transform your negative emotions. If you do not, you will find it impossible to achieve levels of excellence. You will also waste a great deal of valuable energy.

Controlling Emotions

Emotions are not easily controlled. They just sneak up on you and take control. When they take over, the brain shuts down. Rational thinking fails. You tighten up, both physically and mentally, and habitual actions take over. One of the lessons I learned in high school was how uncontrolled emotions can get you "killed."

Although I had been practicing the martial art of aikido for a number of years, I decided to take up kendo, the Japanese martial art of sword fighting. I had been training for almost three years when the instructor announced that we were going to have a match. Our kendo school was going to have the "honor" of competing with a team of midshipmen from Japan who were stopping for a short layover in Hawaii. In essence, we were informally representing the United States in a tournament against Japan.

I was a little nervous when I started, but my first two opponents put aside my fears. The first two out of three points would determine the winner. I won two matches with a decisive 2-0 score. As my third opponent and I were getting ready, he started speaking in Japanese to the person helping him put on his protective gear. I understood a little Japanese and felt smug that I might be getting some inside information. He mentioned how disappointed he was to get such an easy opponent, that he was hoping for someone more challenging.

"Easy," I thought, "I'll show him how good I am."

I was not aware that my rate of breathing had increased as I took a few deep breaths. I felt I was ready to go but didn't realize how much more tense I had become. When the referee signalled us to begin, I saw what appeared to be an easy opening. I moved with lighting speed to score a point on his arm. But as tense as I was, I seemed to be moving at half speed. He easily blocked my blow and scored an easy point to my head.

I realized what had happened at the instant he scored the first point. He probably guessed that, with my Japanese heritage, I understood some Japanese and he had suckered me in. He had taunted me the way Muhammad Ali later taunted his opponents. I quickly tried to calm down, saying to myself, "Relax, slow down your breathing, take it easy and relax, relax . . ."

When the referee signalled us to start a second time, I cautiously waited for him to move. We stood there, swords facing each other, much as the samurais of old had done. Suddenly he moved. I stepped forward and blocked his blow. With a smooth counter stroke, I tried to score a point. He was quick and blocked my wooden sword beautifully. We both stepped back and faced each other again.

He then began taunting me with little movements of his sword while smiling, almost laughing, under his face mask. Suddenly I remembered his stupid comment and I tensed again. That was all he needed. In a fraction of a second, his wooden sword flashed and he scored a point on my arm. The match was over.

Only after the match did the wise words of my martial arts teachers come into focus:

"Never become upset! If you do, you will have lost the real battle. You will have lost, even if you win the fight. The real battle is the battle inside you. The real battle is to first control and then master yourself."

I always thought I knew what he meant, but that day made me realize that knowing something is not enough. It is only when our behavior changes that we have really learned a lesson.

The Tynan Factor

Controlling your emotions is different from simply ignoring them. When you ignore your emotions, you stash them in the depths of your subconscious mind. This "stashing" process provides only temporary relief. In time, and usually at the most inconvenient moments, your emotions spring back to life. Excellence requires a better way of handling your emotions.

To help people, I have developed an effective method for controlling their emotions: the "Tynan Factor." The Tynan Factor is named after an eight-year-old boy named Tynan who showed me how effective this method can be.

One day Tynan arrived at a social gathering with his mother. When he sat down next to me, I noticed that his face was red and there were tears welling in his eyes. I turned to him with a concerned look and asked, "Tynan, what's wrong? You look so upset."

He sniffed and muttered, "My mom made me wear this shirt . . . I'm going to cry."

He had on a bright red shirt. Now, coming from Hawaii where bright aloha shirts are the norm, I thought it looked great. However, I could see that Tynan did not share my sentiment. That shirt was really bothering him.

"Tynan," I asked, "why do you want to cry?"

His eyes grew big and I could almost hear his thoughts. "What? I can cry if I want to. It's my right!"

I probed further. "Tynan, do you want to cry to hurt your mom?"

He nodded, sniffed, and answered, "Yes."

I pointed at his mother and said, "Tynan, look at your mom. She's over there with her friends. She's laughing and having a good time. If you cry, you're not going to hurt her."

His eyes got bigger still.

"Tynan," I continued, "if you cry, the only person you're going to hurt is yourself . . . and you don't want to hurt yourself, do you?"

He shook his head to amplify his, "Nooo . . . "

"Smart people don't want to hurt themselves, and you're a smart boy, aren't you?" I nodded my head.

He nodded in agreement as he said, "Yes."

Within five minutes, Tynan was again in control of his emotions. He was up and playing with the other kids, talking and having a good time. He understood that becoming emotional was only hurting him. His intent may have been to hurt his mother, but his emotions were going to hurt him even more.

In the same manner, your negative emotions and anger cause you to become unhappy. They rob you of possible wonderful experiences and make them terrible instead. Even worse than causing surface unhappiness, emotions create deeper damage. They create stress, the same stress that many doctors now believe is responsible for or contributes to a lot of physical ailments and illnesses.

To control your negative emotions, you must stop yourself immediately. As soon as you notice yourself becoming emotional, stop whatever you are doing and ask yourself, "Whom am I trying to hurt?" The answer is always "the other person." Then ask, "Whom am I really hurting?" The answer becomes "myself."

Sure, you may be able to inflict some pain and suffering on the other person. You may even be able to make him or her suffer over a long period of time. But regardless of what happens to the other person, the person who always suffers is you.

Transforming Emotional Energy

Emotions are simply a form of energy. They are energy associated with a certain person or event. Instead of wasting this energy and getting mad, you must use it wisely. Never waste this energy trying to get even. Instead, use it to better yourself.

When you *transform* the energy into something different, you can release its hold on you. You can use this energy to exercise physically and improve your health, or to read a book and increase your knowledge. You can use it to complete something you have been putting off for a long time. You can transform emotional energy into useful work easily by refocusing your thoughts.

Testing Yourself

The next time you find yourself becoming upset in traffic (a common scenario for almost everyone) test your ability to control your emotions. As soon as you feel your emotions rising, ask yourself, "Whom am I trying to hurt?"

The answer is again the same: you are trying to hurt the other person. You may start yelling, screaming, honking your horn, and even tailgating the person. Yet when he or she finally notices you, his or her probable reaction will be, "What an idiot!"

Have you changed or improved the other person? Probably not. Then ask yourself, "Who just got hurt?" Naturally, the answer is, "I did." In your negative emotional outburst, you became an idiot in the eyes of others. You created stress, the same stress that is detrimental to your health. You really tried to hurt the other person. Unfortunately, the only person you really hurt was yourself.

Of course, there are always a few people who say, "I could hit the person and hurt him or her!" Yes, you could. Then the real pain would begin as you fought both criminal and civil suits in addition to paying for all medical and legal costs. Again, the person really hurt would be you.

Benefits

As the rate of change continues to accelerate around you, the combination of clear vision, flexibility, appropriate decisions, and immediate action will create success. Allowing negative emotions and anger to interfere in that process will severely handicap your ability to take advantage of a rapidly changing environment. Thus opportunities will fly past you, while you remain upset and grounded.

Your ability to control your emotions will improve with practice. Even if you see no real results from your first attempts to control your emotions, you must not give up. Remember that improvement in any area of your life is the natural result of a lot of practice. No one is born a super athlete or a fantastic artist. Similarly, no one was ever born with the ability to control their emotions completely. Control comes through repeated, positive practice.

As soon as you feel yourself becoming angry, stop for a moment. Immediately ask yourself, "Whom am I trying to hurt?" Now answer the question! Remember that every attempt is another step in the right direction. Practice controlling your emotions until it becomes automatic.

Handling Negative or Angry People

In the real world, other people are also unable to control their emotions. They can become upset or even angry for a lot of different reasons. When people become angry and direct that anger toward you, you have to be able to handle all that negative energy.

In the martial arts, I was taught *never to oppose* a force directed at me with another equal and opposite force. Instead, the key to aikido is to avoid a confrontation and move in harmony with the force. When I do that, I can redirect that force where I want it to go.

In the same way, when confronted by an angry person, you must maintain your cool. You must not oppose that negative emotion with your own negative emotion. Remember, the person is angry not at you, but at your behavior or the behavior of others. You must realize that *you* are not being attacked.

An incident involving negative energy occurred when I was managing a group of engineers. One of my engineers, whom I will call Brian, stormed into my office.

"This is such a stupid way to do our job. What were you even thinking about when you sent us these procedures? There is no way this is going to work!"

My ego was under attack. I could have reacted as many people do and shouted back, "It's not stupid. It's the right way. I'm just following regulations. I'm the boss. You just do what you're told to do!"

Then Brian would have yelled again and I would have yelled again, and nothing would have been accomplished. Both Brian and I would have been angry, and productivity would have been reduced for both of us (and probably for everyone else in my department). He would have looked for ways to make me "wrong" while I probably would have done the same to him. Nothing beneficial would have come from the confrontation.

So instead of confronting him, I said, "You know Brian, you're probably right. Now, tell me why this is so stupid."

He began explaining what was wrong with the procedure. After he was finished, I said, "You're right, Brian. This procedure is dumb. I guess I wasn't thinking too clearly when I tried to comply with the latest regulations. Is there any way you can modify that procedure and come up with a better one?"

"In my sleep I can!"

"Great. Thanks for pointing out my mistake. I will really appreciate it if you can modify this procedure."

I did not oppose Brian's anger. Instead, I agreed with him. As soon as I did, his force could no longer be directed at me. How could it, since I was now on his side? He actually needed me because I was supporting his position.

Then I took his negative energy and guided it to solve the problem. I simply asked him to provide a better solution. Now his ego was on the line. When he called the procedure "stupid," he insinuated that he could easily do a better job. I had taken Brian's negative energy and channelled it into something constructive.

We can do this in most office situations. Naturally there are a few extreme cases in which this procedure will not work, but in most cases, simply flowing with the emotional energy and redirecting it works wonders.

Chapter 15
Step 5: Innovate (behavior)
Stress: Stress Management

The American people are so tense that it is impossible to put them to sleep — even with a sermon.
— Norman Vincent Peale

Stress is an essential part of your life. Every time you do something that changes, challenges, or threatens you, stress automatically results. It is actually impossible to do anything without encountering stress. The simple act of driving to work is stressful. Interacting with your superiors and peers is stressful. Actually, everything you do creates some type of stress.

The people, events, or situations that create stress for you are called "stressors." Your skill in being able to handle the stressors in your life is called "stress management." Some of the more typical work stressors include the following:

- Fear of failure and fear of rejection
- Employment uncertainty, lack of job security
- Tight schedules and/or high quotas to meet
- System and process failure or problems
- Unforeseen delays
- Misplaced information or items
- Peer or management attacks and difficult interactions
- Commuting

When people speak of stress, they normally view it as a bad thing. However, it was not always this way. To be in a state of stress was once considered desirable. This is because stress is the body's natural way of building energy to cope with difficulties. Stress prepares a person to perform at peak levels. Stress was never a problem until people stopped using the energy that stress created to take some kind of action.

Here's how stress energy is created. Whenever you believe you are being confronted with danger or a challenge, your body immediately starts to prepare for the situation. It begins by pumping adrenalin into your bloodstream. In response, your heart begins to beat faster, perspiration flows to cool your body, muscles begin to tighten, and you are now ready for action. This is called the "fight or flight response." At this point, the potential energy in your body is peaking. You are now prepared to deal with the stressor, by either fighting or running away.

Unfortunately, modern social behavior does not always allow you either to fight or to run away. Sometimes your only allowable action is to take no action at all. When this happens, stress becomes a real problem. The energy has no place to go and begins to create problems inside your body. It manifests itself outwardly as a number of physical ailments, including high blood pressure, heart disease, stomach ailments, muscle tension, back problems, and headaches.

Whenever you find it impossible to take any kind of action, you must channel all of that potential energy into some constructive outlet. To accomplish this and thereby make your life more pleasant, you can apply the following four basic strategies:

1. Resolve the stressor.
2. Rechannel the energy into some other project.
3. Release the energy.
4. Prevent the energy buildup in the first place.

Resolve the Stressor

Stress is sometimes the result of an unresolved task. You may feel stress because you failed to do something or did something that you regretted. You can remove this type of stress by resolving the stressor.

For example, a person can resolve a typical stressor such as an unbalanced checkbook. Some people are constantly stressed because they are unsure of their checkbook balance. This is a problem easily remedied by balancing the checkbook more often.

Many stressors can be resolved easily, but instead of taking action, a lot of people simply wait and worry. They should stop wasting their energy on worrying and start channelling that energy into resolving the problem.

Another typical stressor might be an unreliable automobile. The owner of the car can resolve the problem by simply having the automobile maintained. In the same manner, a toothache or cavity can be resolved by a visit to the dentist. Whenever possible, resolve any stressful situation.

Rechannel Stress Energy

Some stressors cannot be resolved directly. Two examples are the potential loss of a job and the death of a close friend. A person cannot force the company to stop the reorganization process or bring a friend back to life. However, the energy can be rechanneled into something new and possibly more constructive.

If you are worried about losing your job, you can prepare yourself. Instead of worrying, you can upgrade your skills and knowledge. You can spend all of that stress energy preparing for your next position.

In the death of a close friend, you can direct your stress energy toward a good purpose. Spending some time and energy helping members of your friend's family will release negative stress energy. You can also spend time helping a charitable organization. It makes little difference which organization you choose.

Taking positive action is a very powerful method of reducing stress. It not only helps other people; it helps you as well.

Release Stress Energy

Because stress is the buildup of potential energy, it is released when that energy is expended. There is a long list of exercises you can use to release stress energy. The following are some of the most effective:

1. One of the fastest methods for releasing stress is the use of music. Music can bypass your thinking mind and penetrate deep into your subconscious mind. There it has the power to release your stress.

   The music you choose should be something that is soothing to you. Select the type of music that relaxes you, and then use it often. I recommend using it as you drive home from work and after any stressful event.

   When you use the same type of music regularly, stress release becomes habitual. Almost as soon as you hear the familiar stress-reduction music, your stress will begin to melt. You will begin to feel better almost immediately.

2. Another very effective method of releasing stress is to slow down your breathing. The more slowly you breathe, the more relaxed you become. This stress-reduction technique is especially effective when you are face-to-face with a difficult person. First become aware of your breath. Then slow down your breathing. The more slowly you breathe, the more you will be able to control your stress levels.

   No matter what happens, keep breathing as slowly as you can. Keep reminding yourself, "The more slowly I breathe, the lower my stress."

3. Physical exercise is a great way to reduce stress. Stress prepares you to fight or run away. It motivates you to take action, but the type of action does not matter. Because physical exercise is an activity similar to fighting or running away, it quickly releases the tension created by stress.

   All physical exercises are effective. Jogging, walking, swimming, and dancing are beneficial. As long as the exercise causes your body to move and release energy, it serves as an effective stress reliever.

4. Humor is another wonderful way to release stress. Anytime you can laugh out loud, you release stress. So try to discover ways of adding humor to your life. Any humorous movie or television program that makes you laugh is an effective stress reliever.

5. The final technique is simply to take a break. Take a moment, go off by yourself, and sit quietly somewhere. Take a nap or enjoy a view for a moment. All of these will help to release stress energy.

Prevent Stress Energy Buildup

The best strategy is to employ techniques that prevent the buildup of stress. The following methods work best if they are practiced before the onset of stress:

1. People are sometimes stressed because they strive for perfection. Salvador Dali said, "Don't worry about perfection, you're not going to reach it." If you try to be perfect, you *will* fail. You will then have only stress to show for your efforts.

   Instead of striving for perfection, strive for a high and sustainable quality level. Perfection is for God to achieve. You should be satisfied with simply doing your best.

   Too often we allow others to pressure us into striving for perfection. Take back control of your life and accept that doing your best is really good enough. Then you will have no guilt or regrets.

2. People often become stressed because they impose unreasonable time requirements on themselves. If you have a tendency to do this, stop it! Re-evaluate your priorities, and place reasonable time requirements on top-priority items.

3. Another method of preventing stress is the practice of meditation. Actually, meditation not only prevents stress, but it also helps to remove it.

   Although meditation is a part of some religions and spiritual practices, I am not suggesting it in that context. Meditation has nothing to do with a particular posture or position. It is simply the silencing of your thoughts. When your thoughts become silent, even if it is for less than a minute, stress is being released.

Meditation or silence works because the true cause of stress is within your mind. Your thoughts create stress. When your mind becomes silent, stress is no longer possible.

A lot of documentation supports the benefits of meditation. Two examples of benefits are the reduction of blood pressure, and the prevention of headaches. If you can silence your mind for a few minutes each day, these benefits and others can be yours.

Chapter 16

Step 5: Innovate (behavior)

Attitude: The Power of a Positive Attitude

A positive attitude is the most important factor in overcoming any limitations in your life. — Norman Cousins

People's attitudes have a powerful influence on their state of being. Attitude alone can completely alter their performance. *Being able to control your attitude is a powerful tool in achieving genuine professional power and personal excellence.*

When speaking to managers and executives during a seminar, I often ask them, "What would be the productivity increase if your people came to work each day with a positive attitude and kept that positive attitude throughout the day?" About 75 percent of them give answers of between 80 and 100 percent. About half of the remaining answer more than 100 percent.

Just imagine, for a moment, what would happen if a company could increase productivity by 80 to 100 percent? Stockholders would love the company, while magazines would be fighting to write stories on how it achieved that success. Competitors would be envious and would be trying to obtain the company's secrets.

What would happen to you if you were able to maintain a positive attitude every day, throughout the day? Your productivity would rise substantially. You would be looked upon with new eyes. A promotion might become possible. All this from simply being able to attain and maintain a positive attitude.

Changing your attitude is not as difficult as you think, but before we discuss how to change your attitude, you need to understand why anyone should do it. I must address your most pressing question, "What's in it for me?"

Attitude and Experience

Everything you perceive in the world is colored by your attitude. If you have a positive attitude, you will most likely have more positive experiences. Events will appear more positive than they otherwise would have. If your attitude turns negative, all events will appear more negative. In extreme cases, even positive events may become negative. The following diagram shows the relationship between our attitude and our experience.

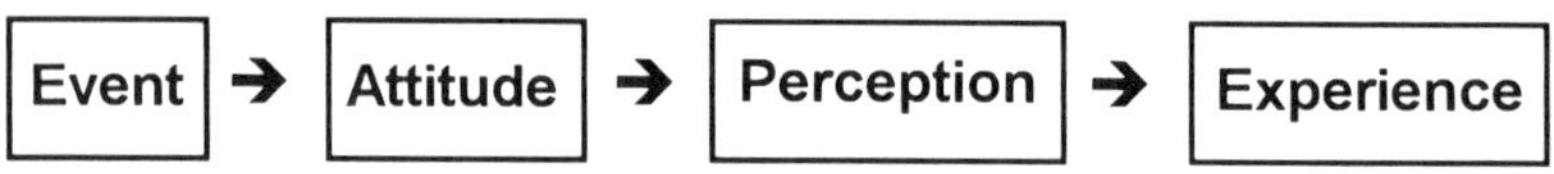

Figure 16-1: How Your Attitude Creates Your Experience

To see how this works, imagine an event that is taking place in your life. Your five senses immediately relay their data to your brain. When the sensual inputs arrive, they are combined and colored by your attitude. Depending on your attitude, what you finally perceive has a value that has been altered by your attitude. This altered perception is your reality.

The more positive your attitude, the more positive your experiences. In the same manner, a negative attitude makes your experience appear more negative. If you can control your attitude, you can control your experiences.

Unfortunately, most of us think that our attitude is not under our control. That is what I thought for more than half of my life. I believed that my attitude was the result of the events that happened in my life. When things were going well, I felt great and my attitude was very positive. When events were really fantastic, I felt wonderful, on top of the world. During those moments, I felt I could do nothing wrong.

Unfortunately, events were not always positive. When difficulty or problems flew at me, my attitude became negative and I began to feel down. As more and more things went wrong, as they periodically did, my attitude became very negative and I suffered terribly. It seemed only natural to conclude that my attitude was controlled by events in my life.

Controlling Your Attitude

Like most people, I was not aware that my attitude controlled my experiences. No one had ever suggested such a concept, but many experiences began to demonstrate to me how a different attitude can totally alter a person's experience.

My stepson, Brad, was a fantastic potter who made outstanding pottery pieces. Like most creative artists, he was also very emotional when it came to his work. If anything happened to one of his pieces, he became upset and yelled at everyone.

One day his sister, Sandi, and I were helping him display his pieces at an arts and crafts fair in Hawaii. We assembled the display shelves and Brad carefully placed his pieces on display. When we were almost finished, Brad went back to the car for a final load.

As Sandi picked up the final support pole and turned around, she accidentally hit one of his pieces and shattered the bottom. I could see the anxiety in her eyes as she said, "Uh-oh, Brad's going to give me heck for breaking this piece."

She paced back and forth as we waited for Brad's return. I stood close by, providing a psychological anchor for Sandi.

When Brad finally returned, she slowly walked up to him and said, "Brad, I'm really sorry but I broke one of your pieces."

Brad looked at his pottery piece and just shrugged his shoulders. He said, "We can't sell it. Just put it in a box and we'll take it back to the car later."

I could see the stunned, almost blank look on her face. Expecting the worst, I was stunned, too. Whatever had happened to that raving artist who lived with us? Her puzzled eyes met mine, but I had no answers. As Brad walked into an adjacent booth to talk to others who were displaying their wares, Sandi made an insightful observation.

"Brad's in love," she said simply, and we found that she was right. Love had transformed Brad's attitude. Looking back I could see the change in his attitude ever since he had met the love of his life.

What a difference a little love makes in a person's life! Before Brad fell in love, his attitude could be terrible. As a result, all of his experiences appeared more negative to him. His attitude created terrible experiences for Sandi. It also created distasteful experiences for me. His negative attitude jaded all of his experiences and made life uncomfortable for himself and everyone else.

After Brad fell in love, everything changed. His attitude was very positive, and this was enough to make his experiences much better. In fact, everything that happened that day was fantastic. It led me to the following conclusion: Attitude controls our perception, which then creates our experiences.

Attitude in the Workplace

Buddy was the head of the drafting division in an engineering firm. He was an excellent draftsperson and did a wonderful job of running his division. Buddy's only problem was his attitude. When management implemented a change, Buddy immediately opposed it. Out of curiosity, I wanted to know how he had acquired his negative attitude.

I asked the "old-timers" in the organization the source of Buddy's problem. It seemed that years earlier, Buddy had asked for a promotion from the chief engineer. Instead of a promotion, the chief engineer ridiculed Buddy by telling him he was not qualified for a promotion. Well, from that moment, Buddy adopted his new, negative attitude. Soon after I met Buddy, the chief engineer and the assistant chief engineer both retired and were no longer associated with the firm.

One day, I was at an office picnic and spoke with the director of engineering, (the new title for chief engineer) about Buddy. The director was well aware of Buddy's situation.

"Gary," he said, "I know how good Buddy is. We would like to consider him for a promotion, but we just can't do it."

"Why not?"

"We can't do it with his attitude. If he were promoted, it would send the wrong message to the other people."

I went back and told Buddy what I had learned. I suggested that he could probably get a promotion if he would only cooperate more and improve his attitude toward management. His reply shocked me.

"Yeah, right!" he said cynically, "and then they'll find another excuse to keep me from getting promoted. I know how they are! They'll promise you anything, but they'll never keep their word. No way, I'll never get suckered again!"

Most of us have had similar incidents. In another department of that organization, John also had an attitude problem. He was a competent engineer whose negative attitude was reflected in his clothing and behavior. He simply refused to follow the accepted dress code or to cut his hair. One day we were playing golf and he was complaining about the fact that he had been consistently denied a promotion. I pulled him aside and said, "Look at the way you talk to people, the way you dress, and the way you look. If you were your boss, would you promote you?"

What I said must have gotten through to him. On Monday he came in wearing a nice dress shirt and a neat haircut. His attitude was totally different. Within two months, his promotion papers had been submitted.

Your attitude creates your experiences. But how often have you seen people carrying big chips on their shoulders? They seem to be oblivious of what they are really doing to themselves. They fail to see that their chips may have become "cow chips," making them look and smell bad! They are the ones who are responsible for "smelling up" their lives.

If you are going to excel, you must gain control of your attitude. Leadership requires that you improve your attitude and that of those who work with you. The CEOs I have spoken to know how people's "normal" attitudes lower productivity. These leaders have taken the first step by identifying a problem. As soon as they can correct it, productivity will increase.

William James, a professor at Harvard, said, ". . . a human being can alter his life by altering his attitudes of mind." It has always been known that a person's life will improve greatly if his or her attitude can become and remain more positive. Unfortunately, no one has ever demonstrated how a person can have complete control of his or her attitude. Schools do not teach people how a simple alteration of their attitude can dramatically alter their experiences and performance.

While in various leadership positions, I realized how important people-related issues are. The technical aspects of management are simple. It is a leader's interactions with people that create most of the real problems. Attitude has always been one of the great interaction problems.

I found the attitudes of the people I managed were more important than their abilities. I could always provide people with necessary skills and knowledge through training, coaching, and educational programs. However, finding someone who had both the right abilities and a positive attitude was rare.

Fortunately, you do not have to *find* people with a positive attitude. Everyone has the ability to *create* their own attitude, but only if they choose to do so. As a leader, you should demonstrate the attitude you expect from others and also provide them with the tools to transform their attitude.

Music to Excite the Spirit

The easiest and quickest way to improve your attitude is through the use of music. Why music? Again, music has the great ability to bypass your conscious mind and penetrate deep into your subconscious mind. Music can change your attitude instantly. The right music can transform your negative attitude instantly and create a positive one, or vice versa.

The type of music to use depends on your personal preference. You should identify the type of music that makes you feel positive about yourself. Some of you may find that classical music or jazz turns you on. Others may get excited by rock or military music. It all depends on your personal preference. When you discover what works for you, use it regularly.

Music has the power to create a lot of different emotional changes. On the negative side, it can create feelings of hopelessness, anger, hate, competition, and fear. Positive music can make you feel hope, joy, power, peace, freedom, and love. Find out how you really feel when you play various types of music. A single piece of music can create a variety of different emotional responses from different people.

To pick myself up, I enjoy the *William Tell Overture* and John Philip Sousa's *Stars and Stripes Forever.* These two pieces excite me. They push my energy up and get me ready to go.

The best time to use music to change your attitude is the first thing in the morning. As soon as you get up, turn on your favorite music. Of course, any time is a good time for music. Especially after a tough day at work, music during the drive home can perform wonders in improving your attitude. After all, you do not want to take a tough day home with you.

Words to Change Your Attitude

Other powerful tools for changing your attitude are your words and thoughts. William James said that you can alter your attitude by altering what you say to yourself. What you think and say to yourself directly affects your attitude. When you think that you are a winner, you begin to feel like a winner. When you think positive thoughts, you feel more positive. Your attitude then becomes more positive.

Of course the thoughts and words on which you focus the first thing in the morning have the greatest effect on you. To help create a lasting positive attitude during the day, start the day with a few positive words to yourself.

Here are a few examples you can use:

> "This is a great day and I'm just as great!"
>
> "I feel fantastic about myself!"
>
> "I'm excited and energized about my future!"
>
> "I'm super-organized and see things clearly!"

When you combine what you say enthusiastically with music, you can create powerful results. Remember how the first song you sing in the morning has a way of bouncing in your head for the rest of the day? In the same way, any words you say with an exciting piece of music can have a powerful effect on you all day.

You must also remember to avoid all negative songs. Songs that say, "I'm a loser," or "Everyone's winning but me," drag you down. Negative songs can pull your attitude down until it, too, becomes negative. When your attitude starts off the day in a negative vein, you tend to remain in that state throughout the day, so avoid negative songs as much as possible.

There are always a few skeptics who think that all of this repetition of positive statements and slogans is useless. So why is it that everyone uses it? Parents repeat encouraging words to their children. Movie directors say positive phrases to actors and actresses. Coaches say positive things to their people and have them repeat it until they begin to believe it. Every coach knows that what you say to yourself has a direct effect on your attitude.

Suppose that you came to work on Monday morning and people began to say the following to you:

"You're looking good today."

"I love your outfit."

"You look like a real professional."

"You did a great job last week."

"You're going to go far in this company."

How would you feel? Would your attitude be good? Would you feel more confident in your abilities? Would you be able to perform with greater efficiency and effectiveness? Of course you would!

Now suppose that the following Monday morning people said the following kinds of things:

"You're really useless in this organization."

"You should do everyone a favor and quit."

"Seeing you has ruined my entire day."

"Boy, are you looking ugly this morning."

Now how would you feel? Would your attitude falter? Would you become upset and angry at others? Would you want to quit or get even with people? What would happen to your performance? Of course your attitude would turn downward.

What other people say to you and what you say to yourself can affect your attitude, for better or worse. So keep saying positive things to yourself to keep yourself positive. Then your experiences will improve and so will those of everyone who comes in contact with you.

Chapter 17

Step 5: Innovate (behavior)

Self-Esteem: Raise Your Self-Esteem

The quality of your life is determined
by the way you feel about yourself.
— Gary K. Yamamoto

Self-esteem is a measure of the way you *feel* about yourself. It is a subjective evaluation of your own behavior relative to what you consider normal behavior. The more your actions outperform your mental standard for normal behavior, the higher your self-esteem.

Do not confuse self-image with self-esteem. They are quite different. In fact, a person can have a high self-image while maintaining a low self-esteem. For instance, a person may think highly of his or her professional or personal skills and have a high self-image, but if the person uses those skills in an illegal or immoral way, he or she may simultaneously have a low self-esteem.

People's self-esteem is based on their actions. The more beneficial or noteworthy the things they accomplish, the higher their self-esteem. The more selfish or negative things they do, the lower their self-esteem.

Improving Self-Esteem

You can raise your self-esteem by accomplishing good deeds. When your self-esteem rises, it may be seen by others as pride. Not the self-serving type of pride, but pride in yourself and in your life. To improve your self-esteem, you simply have to go out of your way to help other people.

My wife and I were in the Caribbean on a week-long cruise. We were having a great time doing a lot of shopping. At one of the ports of call, we decided to buy a few gifts for friends and relatives at the "flea market."

On our way back to the ship, we passed two shacks that had all kinds of trinkets for sale. Between the two shacks squatted a barefooted older man with a beggar's cup. The only clothes he had on were a pair of tattered swim shorts. His arms rested on his knees as he held the begging cup and surveyed the passing crowd. As we passed him, his eyes caught mine for a second, a very long second.

I smiled at him and kept on walking. As we passed the second shack, I suddenly stopped and pulled out my wallet. I took out a dollar bill and handed it to my wife and said, "There's an almost naked man begging between the two buildings. He's got a cup in his hands. I want you to go to him and give him this dollar."

She agreed, took the dollar, and left. After a few moments, she returned.

"What happened?" I asked her eagerly.

"Well," she said, "I found the man you were talking about. I went over and gave him the dollar. He didn't even look at what I put in his cup as he said, 'Thank you.' Then he looked at the cup and saw the dollar bill. Suddenly his eyes got big. He looked up at me again and said, 'Thank you, thank you very much. And God bless you.'"

"How did that make you feel?"

"You know," she thought about it for a moment, "it made me feel really nice and warm all over."

"Yes!" I practically yelled as I clenched my fist, "What a great experience! That man gave you more than money could buy!"

I explained that for one dollar, the beggar had raised my wife's self-esteem. She had experienced what psychologists call a "helper's high." It is that feeling that lifts a person's spirits. Often it lasts throughout the person's life. Whenever he or she thinks about a generous event, that nice, warm feeling will return.

The amount of the gift is not important. A single dollar may give you even greater results than a thousand dollars. What matters is how close you get to the person you help. If you are right there with a dollar, the result for you may be better than it would be if you simply wrote a check for thousands of dollars.

It was also significant that the person my wife helped was not able to repay her. When you help someone who cannot return the favor, life seems to give it back to you. *Besides lifting your self-esteem, helping others often helps you to turn your own life around.*

Always Good Enough

When performing good deeds, remember that all of your actions are always good enough. There is no such thing as too small a good deed. A kind word, a warm greeting, or even a genuine smile may be more meaningful than any amount of money. Your self-esteem is determined by how involved you are with the person you help, and your charitable intent.

A little caveat here: When you have high self-esteem, others may sometimes incorrectly interpret your good feelings about yourself as arrogance. It is all right to feel a high self-esteem, but keep it low-keyed and to yourself to avoid the wrong interpretation by others.

Chapter 18

Step 5: Innovate (behavior)

Self-Image: Maximize Your Self-Image

Each person has a mental picture of his or her ideal self. Moving towards that mental picture is what makes people feel good about themselves.
— Harry Levinson

Your self-image is based on what you think of yourself and is another important factor in your life. It determines the enterprises that you are willing and unwilling to undertake in your life. The greater your self-image, the more adventurous your life becomes.

For instance, imagine that you are an auto mechanic with a poor self-image concerning your professional abilities. In this case, you are not likely to strike off on your own and start your own auto repair business. Instead, you will probably do everything possible to keep your current job.

When you have a poor self-image, it is felt and interpreted by others as timidity or fear. When other people sense timidity or fear from you, they try to take advantage of you. To succeed in life, you need a great self-image.

Having a wonderful self-image makes you more eager and well suited to take risks. You are not be afraid to ask for a larger raise in pay. You may even be eager to go into business for yourself.

When you possess a great self-image, people see you as being more self-assured. This quality of self-confidence is one of the important attributes of leadership. People tend to trust confident people.

A powerful self-image is also perceived as strength and conviction. This, too, is an important attribute of leadership. Achieving professional power requires a positive and powerful self-image.

Measuring Your Self-Image

You have established a unique self-image for various areas of your life. If you rate self-image on a scale from one-to-ten, in which ten is the best, your self-image for one area of your life may be completely different from that for any other area.

For instance, if you are an expert water skier, you may rate yourself as a nine. If you are mortally afraid of public speaking and refuse even to toy with the idea of addressing a large audience, you might rate yourself as a one.

To measure your self-image, pay close attention to your interactions with people. Whenever someone compliments or criticizes you, listen to your reply. It will provide you with hints as to your self-image rating in that area.

For instance, suppose that someone came to you and said this about your job skills: "Wow! What a talented person you are. I have worked with some of the very best in this field, but you are so much better. I have never met anyone as skillful and creative as you."

On a scale from one to ten, you would judge this to be a ten compliment. Now pay attention, because your honest response indicates your self-image. If you agreed with the evaluation and your response was a simple, "Thank you," your self-image is probably a ten.

However, if you found yourself disagreeing with such a high compliment, you can be sure that your self-image is not a ten. If you heard yourself responding, "You know, I don't think I'm that great," or thinking, "I've got you snowed," your self-image is probably less than a ten. In fact your answers are probably saying that your self-image is about a seven in this area of your life.

Whenever you feel you do not live up to a compliment, you are going to try to "sell back" a part of the compliment. You accomplish this by giving reasons and excuses for not deserving a ten. You sell back the extra part of the compliment either orally to the other party or mentally to yourself.

On the other hand, suppose that you just presented a speech and someone gave you the following compliment on your speaking skills: "That wasn't too bad a speech, I guess. No one fell asleep, and most of the people seemed to pay attention to what you were saying. I think you did okay."

This would be about a number five compliment. If you simply agreed with their compliment and said nothing, your self-image in the speaking arena would probably be a five.

However, if you felt that you gave an excellent speech and deserved more, you would not be satisfied with that comment. You would try to buy an additional three or four points. You might find yourself saying to that person, "Are you kidding? I'm a great speaker. I've spoken in front of thousands and have received rave reviews. I even won an award from Toastmasters International last month. Everyone loves my presentations. I don't think you know very much about the speaking business! You've been watching too much television!"

Of course if your self-image were a two, you might hear yourself saying, "Gosh, thank you. I didn't think it was really that good. It was really a simple speech. I didn't think I really got to them . . ." You would try to sell back what you felt you did not deserve.

As people comment on your abilities, listen to your responses. Are you constantly trying to buy back more points, orally or mentally? If you are, you have a higher self-image than people recognize. This is wonderful. Keep improving your abilities and you will soon live up to that higher self-image. If you find yourself selling back those points, your self-image is too low and needs to be built up.

Raising Your Self-Image

There are four basic ways to improve your self-image. They are the following:

1. Improve yourself.
2. Lower the standard against which you measure your performance.
3. Alter your assessment of your abilities relative to the standard image.
4. Build your self-image.

Improving Yourself

One way that you can begin to raise your self-image is by improving your performance. In whatever area you need improvement, you can take the necessary training to improve your physical body, abilities, performance, and results. This is the hard way to improve your self-image, especially when you compare yourself with the best.

Often, no matter how hard you try, you are unable to outperform certain individuals. In every area, there are always those who outperform you. That's a simple fact. They will always make more sales and earn more commissions. They will be more creative, more knowledgeable, write better, speak better, be sexier, have better teeth, or have more fun. No matter what you do, your best will always fall far short of their performance. The solution is simply to do the very best you can.

Lowering the Standard

If you fail to surpass your standard of comparison, the problem may not lie in your abilities and performance. The real problem may be in the standard against which you measure yourself. You may be trying to be the best, when your natural talents and abilities allow you only to be very good. To raise your self-image and to allow yourself to be happy with your life, you must change the rules of the game.

You can raise your self-image by lowering the standard of comparison. You can lower the standard from "the best" to a level of "good." Remember, self-image is a completely mental game. It may sound like cheating or settling for less, but it is not. It is a way of thinking better about yourself and raising your self-image. Comparing yourself to a lower standard will lift your spirits. By doing this, your self-confidence will soar, and this is what you are really after.

Altering Your Assessment

You can also raise your self-image by concentrating on and emphasizing your victories. When others compliment you, simply say, "Thank you."

On the other hand, if you have a negative experience, you can still turn it into a positive one. Think of every mistake as a learning opportunity. If you find what you did wrong and can improve your performance the next time, it becomes a positive experience and a winning situation.

Building Your Self-Image

Because your self-image is the product of your thoughts, you can create a new self-image with new thoughts about yourself. You can alter your self-image through the use of positive and supportive thoughts, words, and actions.

Begin by determining where your self-image is lagging. Suppose that you feel you are not a great leader. When you know what attributes you lack, you can create affirmations to enhance your leadership qualities.

Typical affirmations include the following:

"I believe in myself."

"I am a great leader."

"I am confident in my leadership abilities."

"I always do my best to create winners."

"Tomorrow I will do even better."

Repeat these positive statements to yourself. You can say them out loud or mentally. The more you repeat these statements, the more you will believe in yourself.

Adding Power

To add power to these statements, say them with strong feeling and conviction. You have to believe you really are what you are saying to yourself. So when you repeat, "I believe in myself," you must really feel good about yourself. Under all conditions, avoid the tendency most people have of mentally negating the affirmations later in the day or week.

As in the case with your self-esteem, you must be careful that your new, high self-image does not project too forcefully. A few people may be offended by anyone who feels the confidence that is the product of a powerful self-image. This self-confidence can easily be misinterpreted as a big ego. Build yourself a great self-image, but maintain a quiet confidence and humility when dealing with others.

Step 6
Personal Best
(ability)

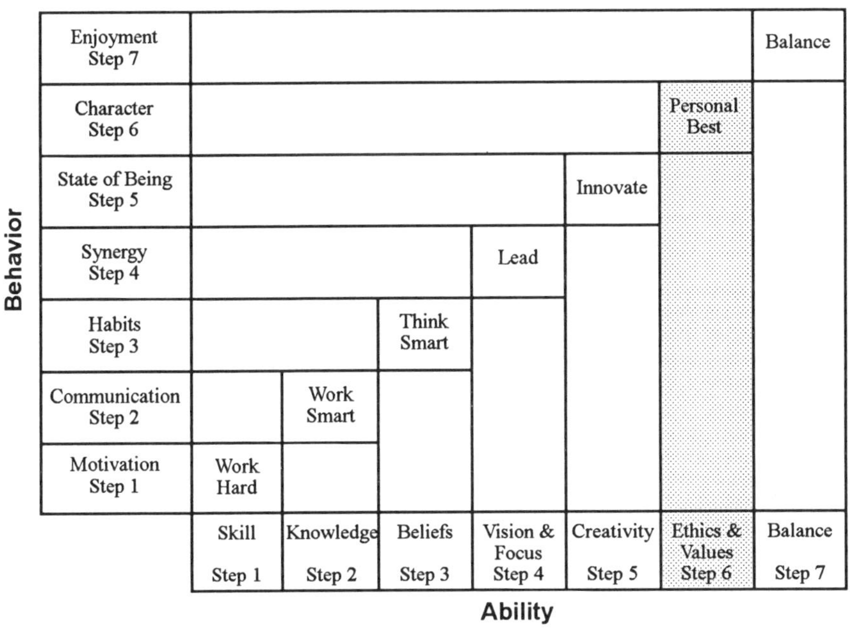

Chapter 19

Step 6: Personal Best (ability)

Ethics and Values: Building Trust

A leader's role is to harness the social forces in the organization, to shape and guide values. — Chester Barnard

Why is there even a need for a discussion of ethics and values? After all, the law requires only that you be law-abiding. However, ethics and values are important in building trust and determining the path you take through life. After all, how many unethical actions can a person perform against you before you stop trusting him or her? The answer is probably — one!

When people do not trust you, it is difficult to get ahead. You may develop a bad reputation which will precede you. To succeed in your professional and personal life, an ethical reputation is invaluable. Guard it fiercely!

A good reputation takes a long time to build. Fortunately the benefits also last a long time. Many years ago, my wife was just starting her first business. After spending several frustrating weeks trying to find her first client, she announced an incentive plan for referrals. She told a few people she would pay a finder's fee from whatever she earned from that particular business transaction.

One day she was approached by a prominent professional in the field, who referred a client to her. She was overjoyed, and in a few days she had made her first deal. She earned three hundred dollars. As a result of her commission offer for referrals, she owed the person who gave her the referral a good chunk of that money. This was money she could hardly afford to part with. Besides, she was not really sure whether he had heard about her finder's fee offer. It was especially difficult when we knew that the prominent professional made well into six figures a year. He would hardly notice the commission that she owed him.

She came to me to discuss the situation. Actually, there was really nothing to talk about. We had a policy that we would always keep our word. We simply had to do what was right. She sent him a check immediately.

Today she is still reaping the benefits of that act. That person knew the sacrifice she had made. He often refers to her as a true professional, someone who is honest and ethical. He has referred other clients to her. Also, she often receives advice from him, and they have developed a great personal friendship and a wonderful working relationship.

Do ethics pay on the bottom line? Only if you want to create more powerful and lasting relationships. If your aim is to develop relationship selling, in which you do repeat business, sterling ethics are a must. If you want to establish referrals, which means that satisfied customers not only love you but also refer others to you, you must maintain world-class ethics.

On the bottom line, you can afford to do only what is ethical. Anything less may one day come back to haunt you. When conducting business, I sometimes ask people or organizations whether I should do business with certain other people or organizations. I often receive comments about something that happened many years ago, comments such as, "I wouldn't! I did business with them a few years ago and they took advantage of me." or "I don't know whether they've improved, but I know I wouldn't trust them."

A few negative comments, spread by word of mouth, through the mail, or across the Internet, can slow down any person or business. A lot of negative comments about ethics are comparable to a stake driven into the heart of a person or business.

Doing Right

Being ethical simply means doing what is right. The term "right" does not mean a set of rules you have to follow. In dynamic human interactions, the right thing to do always seems to change. Different situations, with different people, at different times, change what is "right."

Instead, consider "right" as meaning doing your best. To "do right" means to do what you truly know is right for the situation at hand. Doing right creates win/win solutions for all situations.

When entering into negotiations, we think win-win when we ask ourselves these questions:

"What is the right thing to do?"

"What do I want to get out of this deal?"

"If I were the other person, would this be a good deal for me, too?"

On one extreme, they win big and you lose. On the other extreme, you win big and they lose. Somewhere in between is "win-win" territory, as shown in the following illustration.

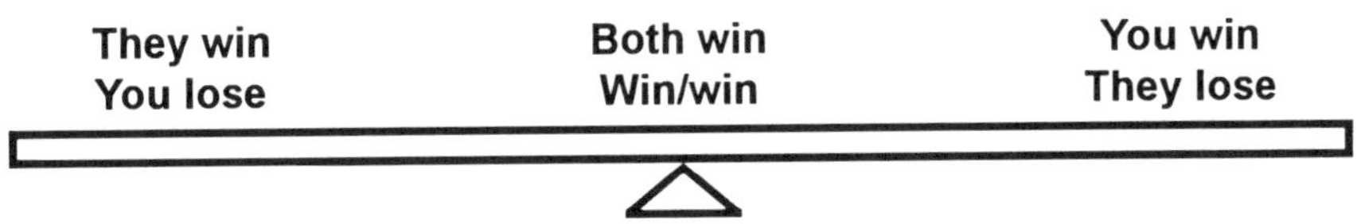

Figure 19-1: Creating Win/Win Situations

In an ethical negotiation, neither extreme is good. If the other side is thinking "win-lose," they will be pushing to take as much as possible and give as little as possible. Ethical negotiation is to arrive somewhere in the middle, preferably a little more toward your side. If they refuse to move from win-lose, you really have "no deal." Break off the negotiations and go somewhere else.

What's In It for Me?

Ethics determines the quality of your life. Each morning, when you have to face yourself in the mirror, do you *really* feel good about your life? If your previous day's behavior was not ethical, you feel it, somewhere deep inside. This feeling, which many try to hide, makes your life less than fulfilling.

Only by embracing ethical behavior will your journey become fulfilling. Only then can you look at yourself and honestly say, "It's great to be alive."

Basic Guidelines of Ethics

Here are some basic guidelines that will help you to conduct yourself in an ethical fashion:

- Do the right thing.
- Say the right thing.
- Have the right thoughts.
- Maintain the right attitude.
- Keep all promises.

The term "right" simply means doing the best you can do today. If you find a better way to do it tomorrow, that will become the new "right" way for you.

A good rule in matters of ethics is to ask yourself, "How would I want to be treated under these circumstances?" The answer to this question will determine how you should treat others.

Values

The way you interact with other people is driven by your ethics, but the decisions you make for you own life are based on your values. In other words, you can choose many different pathways to achieve a goal. Your values determine which road you ultimately take.

For instance, if power and honesty are most important to you, you will journey down one road. On the other hand, if wealth and beauty are most important, you will probably choose another path. If you find yourself consistently taking an uncomfortable pathway, you should re-evaluate your values.

Now you are probably asking yourself, "What are my values?" Most people are not aware of their values. From the list of values given below, take a moment and select, in descending order, the five that are the most important in your life. If there are other values you want that are not included in this list, by all means add them. The five values you choose determine your path through this period of your life.

achievement	adventure	appreciation
approval	beauty	comfort
contribution	control	creativity
energy	enjoyment	freedom
growth	happiness	health
honesty	intelligence	intimacy
learning	love	loyalty
passion	peace	power
recognition	respect	security
sex	stamina	strength
trust	wealth	wisdom

Suppose that three people picked the following lists:

Person 1	Person 2	Person 3
security	power	learning
comfort	wealth	intelligence
peace	freedom	creativity
happiness	respect	contribution
love	energy	respect

Each of these three people will respond to the same situation differently. Their responses will be determined by the values they possess.

For instance, if a dangerous situation were to develop suddenly, how would you respond? If your values were the same as those of Person 1, you would immediately seek some way to protect yourself. If possible, you would avoid the dangerous situation completely. If this were not possible, you would definitely search for a way to establish a peaceful settlement.

If you possessed the values of Person 2, you would immediately try to control the dangerous situation. You would also look for a solution, but in such a way that you would still maintain control of the situation. If a peaceful settlement were not possible, you would not be averse to using force. Also, you would try to profit from the incident.

If your values were similar to those of Person 3, you would probably try to avoid getting physically involved. You might decide to discuss the situation and offer all possible solutions. You would also try to learn as much as you could from this incident.

When you have recorded your top five values, you will understand yourself better. You will see why you naturally respond in one manner instead of another. If money is your highest value, almost every interaction and decision will be seen from a financial standpoint. If peace is your highest value, your interactions and decisions will be different.

If you do not like the way you presently respond to situations in your life, study the values you have recorded and consider modifying them. To do this, simply select a new set of values that are in line with the new responses you desire.

Next, ingrain your new values into your subconscious mind. As you have done before, repeat your new values to yourself with conviction. For example, say out loud, "I desire power," "Happiness is the most important value to me," and "I value my children's future."

Add power by repeating this often. Say it with feeling! Add more power by visualizing yourself acting out your new values. For example, see yourself having and using your power and wealth wisely, or see yourself enjoying a great relationship with your children and guiding them to build their own future.

Select your new values now. Choose wisely, because the values you choose will create your destiny.

Step 6
Personal Best
(behavior)

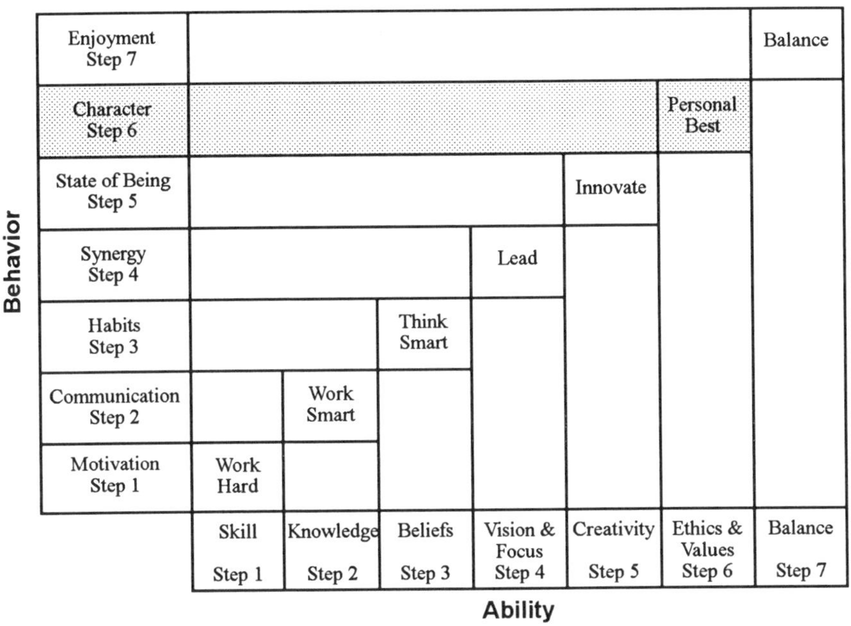

Chapter 20

Step 6: Personal Best (behavior)

Character: When the Going Gets Tough

Never give up, for that is just the place
and time that the tide will turn.
— Harriet Beecher Stowe

By now, you have a good idea of what you must do to transform your life. You have been taught the right abilities and behaviors for success. You now know the right thing to do. The only question that remains is, "Can I continue to do what I have learned, especially when the situation gets tough?"

In this Information Age, obtaining information has not been a problem. People know what they should do to improve their professional and personal lives. Yet somehow they are unable to do it. If people could only accomplish half of what they have learned, they would be fantastic.

For instance, people realize that they should constantly upgrade their skills and knowledge. They may even sign up for a training session or an educational class. But when time limitations, family pressures, work requirements, and other pressures build, they often give it up. Similarly, people also know how they should control their emotions and have a positive attitude — that is, until the next time they become upset.

The ability to follow through is the key factor that separates the knowledgeable from the wise. The fact is, most people do not fail. They simply give up too soon. They literally quit on the eve of success.

The quality of character is your ability to choose the right action and see it through to the end. In spite of hardships and difficulties, you must be willing to take action. When action is initiated, you must also be willing to follow through with your commitments, even when you would rather be doing something else.

Taking Action

Statistics have shown that most people fail to make any meaningful changes in their lives. At a typical seminar or training session, only 2 percent of the people who attend will use any of the information they have gathered to improve their lives. The other 98 percent will take the information home and stack it on a shelf. Their shelf gets smarter, but they do not. They may never look at that information again, until they need the space and throw it out.

They may criticize the presentations as not very informative. They may criticize the presenters, the meeting planner, and even the location. If this 98 percent could just put a single idea into action, the value they would derive from the seminar would increase tremendously. Character is a person's ability to continue doing what is good for him or her, long after others have given up.

To develop your character, you must be willing to take consistent action, even when you feel like quitting. In fact, you must double your resolve to continue, *especially* when you begin entertaining thoughts of giving up. One characteristic separates winners from losers: the loser quits while the winner perseveres and sees it through to the end. Moreover, losers tend to give up at the very time when they should be trying harder.

Consistent Action

The following guidelines will help you to build your character and continue doing the right thing:

1. Because you are trying to create a change that will last a lifetime, this change should be in alignment with some aspect of your life vision. You will be motivated to continue doing the right thing if your actions support your vision.

2. Become a Jedi Knight. I have a Native-American friend named Willie Whitefeather, who is the author of several children's books and loves to share information with them.

   One day I heard some children talking about Willie's presentation, saying they were going to become Jedi Knights, just as he had told them to do. I asked Willie about this Jedi Knight that got the children so excited. He looked at me with shock and said, "You don't know what a Jedi Knight is? Haven't you seen Star Wars?"

   "Willie, I've seen Star Wars. But what does that have to do with becoming a Jedi Knight?"

   "Well," explained Willie, "JEDI is an acronym I created. It means Just Everyday Do It. This is what I tell the kids. If they want to change, if they want to be better, they have to Just Everyday Do It."

   Willie gave me permission to share this with others. This is exactly what *you* have to do. You have to become a JEDI Knight. Simply pick one thing you are going to improve and then commit yourself to *Just Everyday Doing It!*

3. Begin slowly and then build momentum. It is all too easy to become motivated and charge into a new program. Unfortunately, a lot of hard work in the beginning, which is necessary to build a strong foundation, quickly breeds excuses for not doing or following through.

   Begin at a pace you can sustain easily. If you want to increase your knowledge about a particular subject, you can begin by spending a half hour a day studying. If you continue doing this every day for a few years, you will become an expert on the subject. If you are interested in controlling your stress, for example, performing ten minutes of a stress reduction technique, twice a day, will work wonders. As your stress reduction technique become habitual, you will no longer have to practice it consciously. It will become a habit and will occur automatically.

Resist the "I want it all and I want it now" syndrome. Take it easy, one step at a time.

4. Each time you practice something that will improve your life, practice perfect form. Whatever you are trying to accomplish, it is important that you do it correctly each time you do it.

   I really became aware of this when I had a personal physical trainer. He gave me a whole list of exercises for working my entire body. Every few days, the training became more difficult. He increased either the weight or the number of repetitions I had to do. On one particular day, he had me do five extra repetitions. On the last repetition, my muscles were straining and quivering. With my final bit of energy, I pushed the weight up. I took a deep breath and then practically dropped the weight.

   "That wasn't the way I taught you to lower the weight. Do it slowly and with perfect form. Now do it again."

   Grumbling under my breath I strained to lift the weight again. When I finally got it up, I slowly lowered it, IN PERFECT FORM.

   "Good," he said. "You must always do every exercise in perfect form. Do you know why?"

   "No. Why?" I panted.

   "Because the last repetition is where we obtain the greatest benefit. The first few repetitions help a little, but your greatest benefit comes from the last one you do. That's why I insist that *all* repetitions be in perfect form."

   This also applies to changing your life to achieve power and excellence. Every repetition should be as close to perfect form as possible. The last time you practice it is probably more important than the first. When your form is as perfect as possible, the habits you cultivate will be nearly perfect. Do it, each time, as perfectly as you can.

5. Do it especially when you hate to do it. As I said before, *Losers quit on the eve of success.* Successful people always go the extra mile. They are always willing to take action. If you want to achieve excellence and alter your life, you must stop listening to your mental chatter which is trying to justify quitting.
6. Do it with a positive state of being. If you attach a negative state of being to any new activity, the activity will become uncomfortable and you will naturally shy away from it. With a positive state of being, each successful completion will help you to feel even better and boost your motivation to continue.
7. Celebrate all successes. Congratulate yourself every time you do well. Take a moment to pat yourself on the back. Celebrating successes reinforces your determination to succeed and helps you to become better.
8. When you suffer any setbacks, consider them learning opportunities. What did you do wrong? What can you do differently that will help you to avoid repeating the last mistake? Learning not to repeat a mistake definitely puts you on a higher level than those who failed and gave up completely.

Overcoming Resistance

If you find it difficult to take action in the first place, ask yourself the following questions:

1. Is the action I desire in line with my vision? If not, can I align it with my vision?
2. Am I motivated to take action now? If not, can I build motivation by focusing on the positive? Can I gain motivation through the assistance of someone close to me?
3. Does the action go counter to any of my beliefs? If it does, change your action until it is in line with your beliefs.

4. Does the action go against any of my values? If it does, change your action so that it is in alignment with your values.

Developing the right character is the highway to success. Being able to finish what you begin creates winners.

Step 7
Balance
(ability)

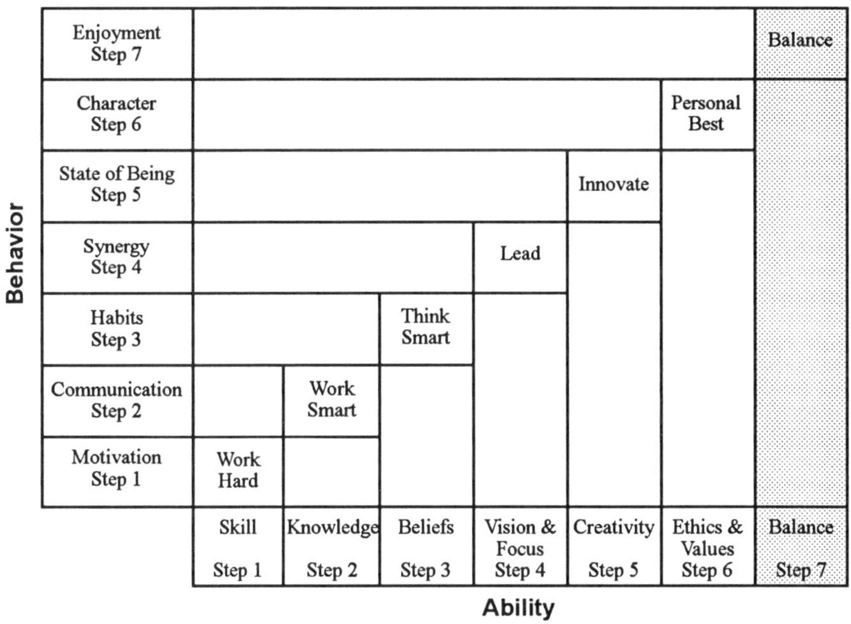

Chapter 21
Step 7: Balance (ability)

Balance: Getting More Out of a Twenty-Four-Hour Day

When I look back at my experience of being confronted with death and ask myself what, in that hour, were the memories I treasured, I have little difficulty in answering. I cared not at all for my personal success . . . What I did care about were the thoughts that I had made a few happier, that I had done a few kindnesses, that I had won some love.

— Arthur Christopher Benson

Psychologists have always been concerned with the impact of technology on people's lives. In the 1950s, their primary concern was how technology would free up people's time, that the four-day work-week would become the norm. They also postulated that the primary problem people would have to face by the turn of the century would be finding something to occupy their leisure time.

Well, so much for dreamers and fairy tales! The average person's life has become anything but leisurely. If anything, people's lives have become a mad rush to keep their heads above water. With corporate streamlining, job demands and stress, family obligations, and other requirements on their time, it is becoming increasingly more difficult for people to balance their lives. Most are overbooked, overstressed and overburdened. With more and more demands on their precious time, they feel boxed in. Whatever happened to those "good old days," when people had to concern themselves about how they would be spending their spare time?

The reality of daily living is now apparent. The trend line is not headed in a positive direction. Instead of having more spare time, people have less and less. Instead of working fewer hours, they are spending more time working than ever before. In fact we seem to have hardly any time for family and friends anymore.

Is the concept of actually balancing your life a myth, a foolish game played by psychologists and authors? Or is there actually a way of creating some sort of balance in your life?

One technique that many time-management experts teach is to prioritize one's life and do only what is most important. People have been attempting to do that. When I survey these people, they tell me it is not working. One woman stated it so clearly when she said, "I prioritize my work and my personal life. I have my 'must do' list, my 'would like to do' list, and my 'if I have some time to do' list. But what do you do when you can't even get to all the 'must do's?'"

For most people, the plan of action is to do, as quickly as possible, what they *absolutely must* do. Then they will try to squeeze in something enjoyable in the remaining time. Unfortunately, what usually remains is almost no time at all. Only a few of their highest priorities are accomplished, and they remain frustrated with their lives.

If you are committed to balancing your life, you need a different strategy. However, before you can create that strategy, you need to understand where you are presently spending your time.

Eight Major Activity Areas

I have identified eight major activity areas in your life: work or career, relationships, family, fun and play, self-improvement, health, sleep and rest, and spiritual growth. Each of these is important to your general health and well-being.

To see how you can balance your life, assign a priority number (from 1 to 8) to each of the categories in the table below. For example, if family is your highest priority, place a "1" next to family, under the category "priority."

	Priority	No. of Hours	+ or - Hours
Work or Career	________	__________	_________
Relationships	________	__________	_________
Family	________	__________	_________
Fun and Play	________	__________	_________
Self-Improvement	________	__________	_________
Health	________	__________	_________
Sleep and Rest	________	__________	_________
Spiritual Growth	________	__________	_________
Total hours		__________	_________

When you have finished assigning your priorities, determine how many hours per week you presently spend on each activity area listed. To help you determine this, you may wish to keep a record of what you do on a typical day. In Appendix A: "Estimated Time Spent On Each Major Activity," found in the back of this book, record how you spend your time in fifteen-minute segments. Otherwise, you can guess at the number of hours you spend on each activity every week.

List the total number of hours spent on each activity during an average week in the table above. Remember, a week has only 168 hours.

Now place the number of hours you have recorded in the "Chart of Activities" on the next page. This chart offers you a graphic view of how well your life is balanced. From this, you can begin to juggle time in order to balance your life.

If you are like most people, your chart will be completely out of balance. Much of your time is probably spent at work. A large part of the remainder is probably spent sleeping. Many of your other activities most likely receive little or no time allotment at all.

This is your moment of truth. You may *say* that something is your top priority. If, however, the chart reveals that you are spending insufficient time on a high-priority area, changes will have to be made. To increase the number of hours you spend in one area, determine which of the other areas you are going to decrease. Remember, there are still only 168 hours in a week!

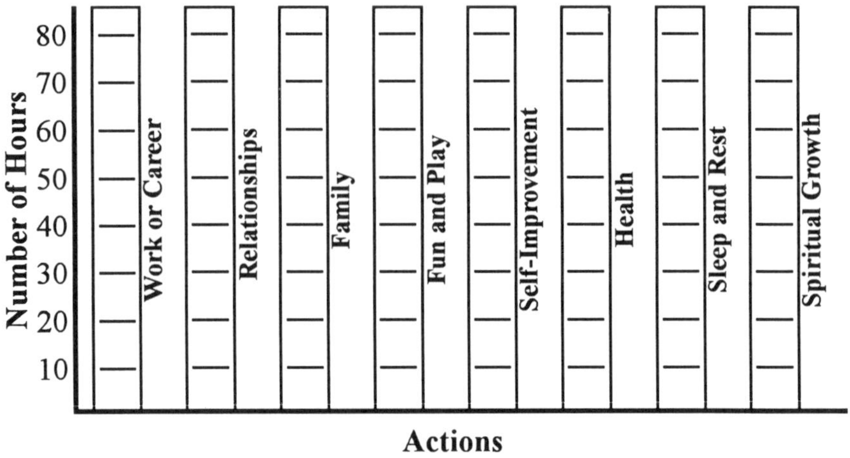

Figure 21-1: Chart of Activities

If you decide to increase the number of hours you spend with your family by six hours, you must decide where these six hours are going to come from. Which activity will suffer so that you can have an additional six hours with your family? Will it come from work time? How will you manage that? You might decide to take it from the time you spend sleeping. Unfortunately, if you are like most people, you have already used all the sleep time you can possibly spare.

True Balance

Although the term "balance" implies that you have an equal number of hours for each major area, this appears to be impossible. For one thing, most people spend a minimum of nine hours at work, including the commute and meal times. They also spend eight hours a day sleeping. These two activities total 101 hours. Only sixty-seven hours remain for everything else. Time, our most precious commodity, seems to vanish into thin air.

According to a recent poll, the average working person has about two and one-half hours of discretionary or free time each day. This is appalling because your discretionary time determines the quality of your life. How can we balance our lives with this challenge?

The average working woman has it worse. She has less than two hours a day of discretionary time, and her free time usually occurs somewhere between 10 p.m. and midnight. When I share this statistic with women, many agree that it is true for them. Others say that they have not yet found their two hours per day!

My office manager mentioned that her friend has a job and two children. The woman gets up at four in the morning for her free time. She has about one and one-half hours before her husband wakes up. Right after that, the children charge out of bed and the rest of her day is completely booked. It reminds me of what Henry Kissinger once said: "We cannot have a crisis. I'm already fully booked." Everyone, it seems, is now fully booked.

Creating More Time

What if there were a way to create more time in a day? Would you like that? Of course, you are probably asking, "What magic do I have to perform to accomplish this?" No magic, just a *psychological shift.* I call this "piggybacking activities." In piggybacking, you allow one activity to become different activities simultaneously. This allows one activity to serve double or triple or even quadruple duty.

As an example, you can piggyback the time you spend at work. For most people, work is work. However, work is not just work if you are also having fun. Can work become fun? Can you actually have a good time while working? Yes!

Have you noticed how enjoyable your workday becomes when you are having fun? Time seems to flash past you. Before you know what happened, the day is over. At the end of the day, you are not tired. In fact, you probably feel energized. What a difference a little fun can make in the quality of your life!

Work can become enjoyable if you decide that it is possible to enjoy yourself. You can search out moments of fun and focus on them, thus helping to relieve even the most stressful moments. As discussed before, reality is created and altered through your mind. When you can change your point of view and concentrate on the enjoyable aspects of work, you can really enjoy working. You can enhance your experience by using your mental "spin doctor" to alter your experiences. If you can make even a few hours of a workday a time of "fun," you can alter your chart of activities. You can get more than 168 hours from a week.

The list below shows you some ways to view one activity in various ways so that it serves more than one purpose:

Work	fun and play self-improvement spiritual growth
Relationships	fun and play self-improvement spiritual growth health
Family	self-improvement spiritual growth health
Fun and Play	family self-improvement health sleep and rest spiritual growth
Self-Improvement	relationships fun and play health spiritual growth
Health	fun and play self-improvement spiritual growth
Sleep and Rest	self-improvement health
Spiritual Growth	relationships family fun and play self-improvement health

Suppose that you could piggyback three hours of work with fun. From nine hours at work, you could write down nine hours for work and three hours of fun. You just made nine hours into twelve hours.

Further suppose that, in the same day, you experienced a tough situation at work. For two hours, you handled a problem with a co-worker and learned how to create a win-win situation. You just piggybacked two hours of self-improvement into your workday. Your nine hours at work is now up to fourteen hours of experiences.

Another piggyback situation is to use your time at work for spiritual development. Then you can practice some of the powerful, universal spiritual principles you know, such as faith, truth, love, joy, peace, and forgiveness. In this manner, you can actually increase the time you spend on spiritual development in your chart of activities.

Yes, this is a mental game. If I could reduce it to a short statement, it would be, *"It's not what you're doing with your activities, it's what you can combine them to become."* It is possible to get more than twenty-four hours out of a day, and your life will be more fulfilling if you do. Balancing your life and piggybacking is the first step. However, to make full use of your time, you also have to energize yourself.

Plugging the Black Holes

To help you get more out of your life, you must increase your energy. You can begin by minimizing activities and situations that drain your energy. The following are the most common sources of energy drains:

1. Negative people
2. Other people's problems
3. Post-vacation overload
4. Junk mail

Negative People

Negative people drain your energies. They cause you problems, upset you, or simply bring down your state of being. Whenever possible, insulate yourself from negative people. There are four ways to accomplish this: help them to change, leave the situation, get them to leave, or rise above their negativity.

Helping people to change is a good thing to do if you are the person's manager or a family member. With these relationships, people will tend to listen. Otherwise, you may find it difficult to change others. They will probably resist what you suggest or even become upset. Attempt to change others only if you are their boss or a concerned family member. Otherwise, your best solution is to give them a copy of this book! Let them learn how to change on their own terms.

Another solution is to leave the company of negative people. Unfortunately, this is not always an appropriate solution. Even if you do find another job or group, there will probably be other negative people in the new group. Finding another group rarely solves your problem.

The last way is to rise above the negativity. This process is often easier than you think. You can simply alter your attitude and become very positive. No matter what the other person says or does, just maintain a positive attitude. You can use uplifting music to keep your attitude up. A positive attitude along with great self-esteem can lift your perception and make all of your experiences more positive.

Other People's Problems

You can choose *not* to take on other people's emotional problems. By this, I do not mean you should not help people. Just do not psychologically take on someone else's problems.

Unfortunately, our society has incorrectly taught us that we must sympathize deeply with other people. This is not really necessary. You can empathize with others, but you do not have to share their anguish, anger, and problems in order to care. If you are too deeply involved, you can be dragged down. When you are sucked into this level of feeling, it becomes difficult to pull yourself up, much less anyone else.

I refuse to sympathize with others and to make their negative emotions part of my experience! However, I am willing to empathize, to understand what they are experiencing. I am willing to help people, within reason. But under no circumstances will I allow myself to become emotionally negative. This is critically important to maintaining my own enjoyment of life and my own positive outlook.

The classic example is a negative close friend who comes to visit you. He pours out his heart and shares all of his problems. You are feeling great and want to help him. You sympathize with him and try to lift his spirits up. When he finally leaves, he will probably feel much better. You, on the other hand, will feel tired and emotionally drained. This happened when you sympathized with him and took on his problems.

Whenever possible, do not allow others to unload their problems on you. You can understand, support, and help others, but you do not have to become emotionally involved. Life is too short! Besides, you have enough of your own personal situations to keep you busy. Do not take on someone else's problems!

Post-Vacation Overload

Post-vacation overload is another source of energy drain. You have probably been told to take a vacation to relieve stress and renew yourself. You schedule a week or two when you can get away and rest. The vacation is great and you really enjoy yourself. You successfully shed yourself of all the cares and worries of work and daily living.

Feeling refreshed, you return to work, only to be faced with post-vacation overload. All of the work that accumulated while you were gone is now piled on top of your desk. No one took care of any of it. You are now expected to handle your usual daily tasks in addition to catching up with the backlog. At the end of the first day, you really need another vacation. You have just been run over by post-vacation overload.

Instead of having this happen to you, devise a plan of action. If possible, arrange with someone to fill in for you while you are on vacation. Others can take care of a lot of the usual workload that does not need your special attention. You can then reciprocate when they go on their vacation.

Junk Mail

Psychologist William James said, "The art of being wise is the art of knowing what to overlook." You must minimize everything unimportant that drains your time and energy.

Junk mail is a source of energy drain. You can minimize the amount of time you spend going through it. To do so, you need an efficient way to sort through all the unsolicited paperwork quickly to extract the gems.

One way to handle mail is the following: establish four "don't know what to do" folders. Sort every piece of junk mail into three categories: useful now, trash, and don't know what to do. Process the useful information by the end of the day. Discard the trash immediately. Place the remaining mail into the first of the "don't know what to do" folders. At the end of the week, pull the next of the four folders forward and use it.

At the beginning of the fifth week, your folders will all be full. Take the oldest folder, throw out all the contents, and then use it for the current week. Why? The thinking is that if you did not go looking for that information in a month, you will probably never need it in the future. If you make a mistake, you can always ask for another copy.

Energizing Yourself

Professional power and personal excellence require that you energize yourself, so that you have the necessary energy to accomplish whatever you desire. The following will help to energize you:

1. Improve your diet.
2. Exercise.
3. Participate in an energizing pastime or high-quality leisure activities.
4. Associate with positive people.

Improve Your Diet

Changing your diet can provide quick results. Instead of choosing one of the complex or painful formulas and diets, a simple way to improve your diet is to adhere to the following rules:

Decrease	Increase
Fats	Fiber
Refined-grain products	Whole-grain products
Processed foods	Fresh vegetables and fruits

Salt	Water
Sugar	Protein
Caffeine, nicotine, drugs	

This diet is really practical and simple. Minimize all fats in your diet. It does not matter whether the fats come from animal or vegetable sources. Fat is fat! Replace it with more foods that are high in fiber.

Minimize all refined carbohydrate sources, such as white flour. Replace them with more whole-grain products that have complex carbohydrates.

Minimize all processed foods, and increase your fresh-food intake. Minimize salt, and increase your intake of water. Replace white sugar with fruits. Finally, minimize all drugs, even coffee and nicotine. Of course, you should consult with your physician to address any special dietary or health requirements.

Exercise

Aerobic exercise can energize you. To help you to remove stress and get your system moving, you must commit to a regular program of exercise. The exercise you choose should be sustained for whatever time feels comfortable. Again, consult with your physician to address any special health requirements.

A few people actually exercise too much. They overdo, draining their energy and leaving themselves feeling tired. This is not your objective. You are training for life, not for competition. You must approach exercise in a sensible manner. If, after you complete your exercise program, you feel very tired and need to rest, you may be overdoing it. The objective of your exercise program is to improve your health and energy level.

Participate in an Energizing Pastime

You can also energize yourself by participating in an exciting pastime or some form of high-quality leisure activity. You can choose fishing, hiking, birding, knitting, or any of a thousand different avocations. The only important consideration is whether this activity increases or depletes your energy. Avoid activities that drain your energy!

Associate with Positive People

Finally associate with positive people. These are the ones whose company you love, the people who make you feel good. No matter what problems they may be experiencing, they are always optimistic that events are going to improve.

To associate with uplifting people, you must also be positive. Otherwise, you may become the drain on their energy battery. Like attracts like. Keep your state of being positive and positive people will be attracted to you.

Step 7
Balance
(behavior)

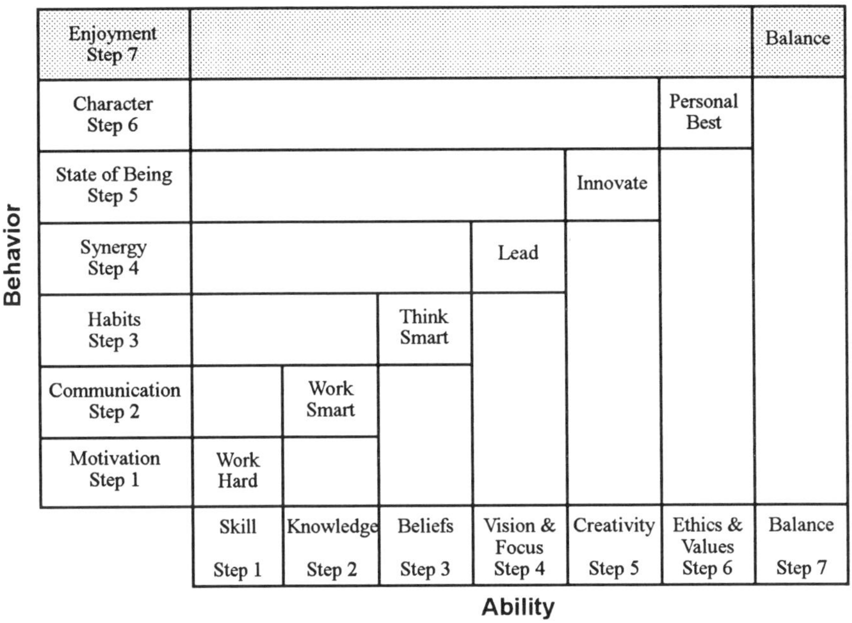

Chapter 22
Step 7: Balance (behavior)
Enjoyment: The Keys to Life!

There are two things to aim at in life; first, to get what you want; and after that, to enjoy it. Only the wisest of mankind achieve the second.
— Paul Pearsall Smith

At the end of their lives, hardly anyone ever says, "I wish I had spent more time and energy at work, applied myself, and achieved more." When asked, most people will admit that they wish they had spent more time with their families. They would have liked to visit a few more places and investigate some different ideas in more depth. They also admit that much of their lives was repetitious and that they wish they had done a few more adventurous and exciting things.

Fortunately, you have an opportunity to avoid that — right now. You can turn your life around and end the repetitious cycle you are living. This is your opportunity to begin enjoying life. But you must start right now!

Enjoying Life

Enjoyment is not what happens to you physically, but how you process it mentally. You can see this when you watch people. Under identical conditions, some people are happy while others are unhappy. Some are having a great time while others are suffering.

One evening, my wife and I were dining in a busy restaurant with a close friend. My wife had just mentioned how cold the restaurant was when the power suddenly went out and the whole restaurant went dark. The waiters quickly brought candles to every table. As we continued to eat by candlelight, I watched how different people responded to the problem.

The couple behind me were upset. The man began to complain about the lighting, as did his wife. They finally told the waiter how terrible the evening had become, got up, and left. This response was the opposite of that of the two couples at the adjacent table. That man said that this reminded him of his camping days, and they began laughing loudly as they told campfire stories.

There were different responses at our table. My wife thought this was the greatest in timing. She joked that God must have heard her complain about the cold and turned the power off, just for her. She also felt that dinner by candlelight was much more romantic. My friend and I were a lot less dramatic. We just continued enjoying the evening, telling stories and eating our meal as if nothing had happened.

Regardless of the situation, people have different responses. Therefore, the event or situation itself does not cause happiness or unhappiness. Events are all neutral. If an event makes you unhappy, the problem is not the event. The problem is the manner in which you mentally process the event. Depending on how you process what is happening, you can make any event more positive or more negative. If you process the event in one way, you can enjoy yourself. If you process it in a different way, you become unhappy.

Suppose that you were totally down on your luck. You had lost your job a while back and were not able to find another. You were down to your last few dollars. You had no money to pay either your bills or your mortgage. On Saturday morning, with one of your last dollars, you purchased a lottery ticket.

That evening, you discovered that you had won the lottery jackpot of twenty million dollars. At that instant, your blues disappeared. You were excited and feeling energized. That evening you called your friends and relatives to tell them the fabulous news. You wanted to cash in the ticket immediately, but you had to wait until Monday morning when the lottery office opened.

Your friends invited you to a party on Sunday morning. You agreed to go and decided to take the ticket with you to show them.

When you arrived, your friends asked to see the winning ticket. You searched your billfold and discovered, to your horror, that the ticket was gone.

You panicked! You emptied your billfold and pockets, but there was no sign of the ticket. You ran out to the car and searched it without any luck. You immediately drove back home and searched the whole house for the ticket. The ticket was nowhere to be found. You suddenly had to face the reality that the ticket was lost. The reality that you were no longer a millionaire hit you. You were really down in the dumps.

Later that evening, your daughter came in and saw you looking very depressed. She told you to cheer up, that you were a multimillionaire and should be happy. You broke the news to her and told her that you had lost the lottery ticket. Instead of crying, she laughed and pulled the winning ticket out of her purse. She had had it all the time. She had taken it with her to show off to her friends. Suddenly you were happy again, for you were a millionaire once more.

The next morning you rushed to the Lottery office. There you were informed that this was a freak drawing. You were only one of a hundred winners. Instead of receiving a million dollars a year for twenty years, you would receive only ten thousand dollars a year. The amount would be reduced further by the tax on that money. As a result, you were no longer feeling as good as you did before.

What happened? You had gone from feeling down, to up, to down, to up, and finally back down again. What had really changed? At no time were you ever any different. The only difference was how your mind perceived the world and how you were reacting to it. When you thought things were going well, you felt good. When you thought things were not going well, you felt bad.

Just as events are neutral, so are material things. What is great to one person may be terrible to another. An old bottle would be a valuable find to a bottle collector. The same bottle would be simply trash to the ordinary person.

What is a wonderful gift in one situation may become terrible in another. To most people, receiving a bag of gold is seen as a great gift. To a person struggling to keep from drowning in the ocean, a bag of gold is the last object they would want weighing them down.

Things and events do not have any intrinsic power in and of themselves to create enjoyment. Instead, your enjoyment is under the control of your mind. When you are able to control your mind, you have the power to control your enjoyment.

Controlling Your Enjoyment

There are three keys for increasing your enjoyment of life. They are very effective, and they will work every time. They are as follows:

1. Lower expectations.
2. Reduce desires.
3. Handle tragedy.

Lower Expectations

Almost all of us have been told to have high expectations of ourselves and everyone else in our lives. You have probably been taught that the higher your expectations, the higher your achievement. The instructors probably added that you can achieve maximum results if you become emotionally attached to the expectation and the results you achieve. In a business sense, having high expectations seems to be effective in pushing your career forward.

Are you emotionally attached to high expectations, such as to a level of sales you must achieve or a promotion you must receive? If you are, you may be setting yourself up for future problems, for you will eventually become unhappy, frustrated, even angry with yourself or with others in your life.

Let us use Les and Mo as an example. The boys were from two different families and were about to graduate from high school and enter college. Les expected very little in the way of a car from his parents, who were not doing too well financially. Although he had asked them for a car, he expected nothing.

Mo, on the other hand, had high emotional expectations. His parents were very wealthy, and they both drove BMWs. He had asked his father for a BMW, to which his father had replied, "We'll see."

On graduation day, both boys received identical gift vehicles, which cost much less than a BMW. Les was ecstatic to possess any vehicle. He could hardly wait to get behind the wheel and show it off to his friends.

Mo, however, was visibly upset. This vehicle was not worthy of him. After all, his parents had said many times that the only really worthwhile vehicle was a BMW. Mo did not really want to drive his new car, especially because he had told his friends that he would be getting a BMW.

The difference in reactions between Mo and Les demonstrates the difference in their expectations. Mo, with his high expectations, had created the conditions that would eventually guarantee his unhappiness and suffering.

This is how it works. Mo's high expectations allowed only two possible outcomes: his expectations would be fulfilled or not. If they were fulfilled, he would feel wonderful and elated. However, because he already expected what he received, his euphoric feeling would not last very long. In fact, it would rise and then quickly fall back down to neutral. This is illustrated by the top line in the figure below.

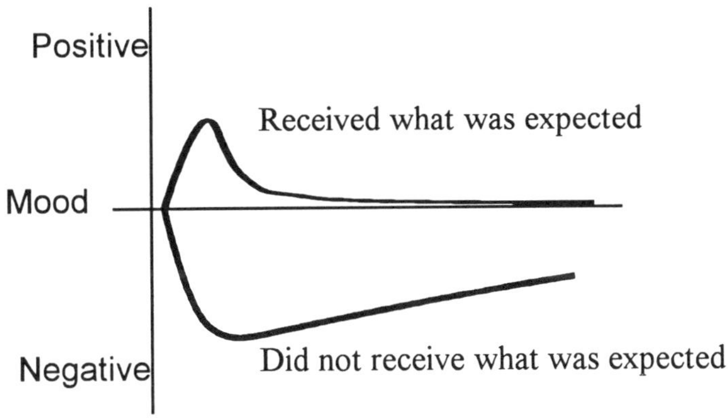

Figure 22-1: Moods with Expectations

Of course, after receiving his BMW, he would raise his expectations, wanting a better model of BMW. Naturally, there would come a time when Mo's expectations could no longer be met and he will be upset and unhappy. His energy would drop down and remain there for a long time. This mood change is illustrated by the lower line in the figure above.

In general, having high emotional expectations is not a good way to live. When your expectations are met, you will feel good for a short time and then drop back down to neutral. If they are not met, you might enter into a state of frustration or even depression. Emotionally, there is little benefit to having a high emotional expectation.

Les, on the other hand, did not have any expectations. If you do not have any expectations, or any emotional attachment to your expectations, you will respond in a manner similar to Les, When Les received his vehicle, he was ecstatic. He had expected nothing, and he loved what he received. This enthusiastic feeling will remain for a long time, as illustrated by the top line in the figure below.

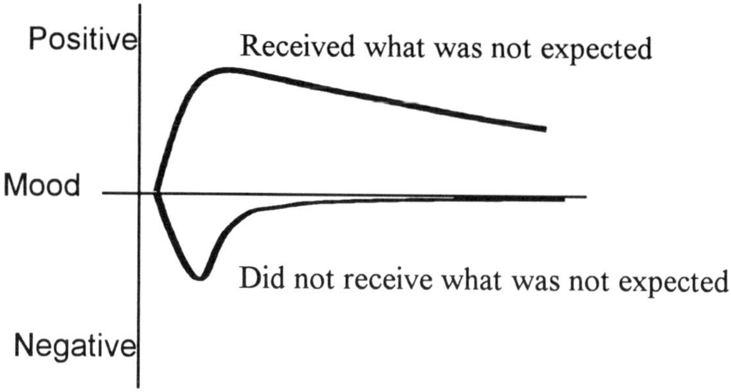

Figure 22-2: Moods without Expectations

If Les had not received anything at all, he would not have felt too bad. After all, he had not expected anything. He may have begun to feel a little low, but only for a short time. He would have bounced back up to neutral quickly. *Thus the key to happiness is your ability to remove any emotional attachment to your expectation.*

Because your expectations are similar to your goals, is it possible to have goals without being emotionally attached to their achievement? If you simply set your goals and did your best to achieve them, with no emotion attached, you would not be upset if you did not achieve your goals. If you did achieve your goals, you would feel wonderful and remain so for a long time. Therefore, it is good to have goals. What you have to do is avoid any emotional attachment to them.

Can you live without any emotional attachments? You will have to find this out for yourself. In my own life, I know it is possible! I have been able to minimize almost all emotional attachments. I enjoy life as I would a game. I work toward achieving my goals without any strong emotions. If I fail, I am not upset. If I attain my goals, I feel wonderful!

Reduce Desires

Just as your expectations placed a limit on your enjoyment, your emotional desires do the same thing. However, unlike expectations, which tend to have an upper limit, desires have no limit. Again, the more intense your desires and the greater your emotional attachment to achieving your desires, the lower your chances of enjoying your life.

Perhaps this is why most religions suggest that people place a limit on their desires and expectations. The greater a person's desires and expectations, the more dissatisfied he or she becomes with life. The wise way to live, work, and enjoy your life is to place a limit on the emotional attachments to your desires and expectations.

Handle Tragedy

Sometimes events occur that you cannot mentally justify. A tragedy strikes because of a freak happening of nature. People you know and love get sick, are injured, or die. How can you maintain yourself and enjoy life in light of these events?

These types of events occur all the time. An earthquake hits and creates tremendous suffering. Lightning strikes, volcanos erupt, bridges fall, and airplanes crash. Hundreds, sometimes thousands of people are killed. When tragedy happens, surviving relatives search for someone to blame.

An earthquake took place in Kobe, Japan, in 1995, killing thousands. As reporters talked to the survivors, the Japanese people did not appear to be very upset. They almost shrugged off the incident and continued doing their best. When asked what they thought of the incident, a few of them replied, *shooganai.*

I grew up understanding this attitude. Shooganai is a Japanese word that means "it could not be helped." The situation may be bad, things may be tough, but often there is nothing anyone could have done to prevent it. If you can maintain this attitude, you can minimize your unhappiness. It is an attitude that can keep you from becoming upset when nothing can be done.

This concept is very Oriental. It is one way in which the Japanese people keep themselves centered during tragedies. They remain calm because the shooganai attitude helps them maintain peace when dealing with the realities and changes that occur in life.

Although it is good to remain calm during difficult times, is it still possible to grab some of the gusto of life? After all, this chapter is about enjoying life. This is the topic of the next section.

Life's Greatest Secret

Life's greatest secret is obvious. When I first heard it so many years ago, it sounded almost funny. But the greatest secret is simply this: *you can be only one thing at a time.*

This means that if you choose to be happy, you cannot choose to be anything else. If you are happy, you cannot choose to be frustrated. It is impossible to be happy when you are frustrated. The two states cannot co-exist. So each time you find yourself becoming frustrated, stop!

If you wish to be happy, you cannot choose to be jealous, angry, afraid, or confused. Nor can you choose to be upset, envious, or sad. You must always choose happiness, no matter what is happening to you.

What do you choose for your life? Do you choose to be happy and enjoy life? Do you choose love and peace of mind? Would you like to choose love, joy, and peace of mind as I did? Whatever you choose, you must commit to that — and that alone. You must do it without wavering. When you can do that, love, joy, and peace of mind will be yours!

Chapter 23
Summary
Transforming Your Life

A journey of a thousand miles begins with the first step. — Confucius

You now have the seven steps necessary to transform your life and achieve permanent professional power and personal excellence. As you improve yourself with each of the steps, your career and personal life will be profoundly transformed. The process will not be difficult.

This chapter lists the most effective strategy for creating a long-term, permanent change in your life. Details of how to achieve each tactical point, such as motivation, state of being, vision, and so on, are found in the individual chapters of this book. You can begin by becoming motivated about creating a change.

Motivation

Remember that the primary motivators in life are pain, pleasure, and the price of change. Identify the pain of remaining "here" where you are. Is it painful enough to motivate you? If not, mentally exaggerate the pain so that it seems more acute.

Next identify the pleasure you will gain by moving "there." Be sure that the pleasure is great enough to entice you to change.

Finally, become clear about the price of change (amount of work) you can expect. There is no room for surprises as you work to change yourself. Be aware of what will be involved, and mentally prepare for and commit yourself to the work ahead. You will find it well worth the effort!

State of Being

Before you attempt a vast transformation of your life, learn how to create and maintain a positive state of being. Remember, your state of being determines your experience. With a positive state of being, even bad experiences will not appear quite as terrible. At the same time, positive experiences will appear to be even more wonderful. Therefore, carefully maintain a positive state of being at all times.

Vision

Your present life is the result of your existing vision. If you dislike what you are experiencing, you need a new vision. Ask yourself, "What do I want to achieve in this life?" This is probably thc most important question you can ever ask yourself. If your vision is small, your achievements will be correspondingly small. If you can raise your vision to great heights, great things become possible.

Remember that life is more than your career or your profession. It is also about your personal life. The basic qualities that everyone seems to want, consciously or otherwise, have always been love, joy, and peace of mind. Almost everything you can envision or desire is a form of one of these three. Be sure to include some form of love, joy, and peace of mind in your new vision.

Values

Your present life is also the product of your present values. The values you have now are probably the same ones you had when you were in grade school. They were given to you by your peers, teachers, parents and family, and the media. The path you choose for obtaining your vision is largely determined by your values. If you do not like the results, it may be time to select a few new values.

Especially in positions of leadership, people must identify and live high values. Chester Barnard, past president of New Jersey Bell, said that a leader's role is to shape and guide the organization's values. Post your values in a conspicuous place to remind yourself and everyone else what is important.

Beliefs

What would you believe about yourself if you were already living your vision? Put your answers into simple, affirmative statements, and write them down. These might include, "I am successful," or "I am innovative." Repeat these statements every day, both mentally and out loud. The more you repeat these, the stronger they will be etched into your subconscious mind. Your beliefs are exactly what you create in your life.

At the same time, stop saying negative things about yourself. All negative beliefs that are reinforced regularly will prevent change. Those who say, "I never win anything!" are not only stating a fact, they are also supporting their future tendency never to win anything.

Those who tell everyone, "Oh, I am always winning something," will keep on winning. Remember, *this is a self-fulfilling universe.*

Habits

Acting "as if" does a lot of good. If you think you are "there," and you start acting as if you are "there," it is only a matter of time before you actually get there. Lao Tsu said that manifesting or bringing objects or situations into reality is the process of "be, do, then have." "Be" is to believe you are there. "Do" is to do the right things to get yourself there. "Have" is the result.

Ethics

In all your dealings, go beyond legal to ethical. Do what you think is really the right thing to do. Remember, you have to live with yourself. It is a delightful feeling when you can look at yourself in the mirror each morning and truly like the person you see.

Having high ethics may or may not increase your professional results. However, a high standard of ethics improves your personal state of being and people tend to trust you more.

Skills

Identify any additional skills you will need when you get "there." Then commit the necessary time and funds to improve your skills constantly. Remember that every position requires a lot of different abilities.

Knowledge

Education is the path through which you can increase your knowledge. You can achieve this through either formal education or a self-education program, such as one that makes use of books, audiotapes, videotapes, and seminars. Without constantly improving your knowledge, you will be moving backward.

There is another, more effective means of expanding your knowledge. Henry Wadsworth Longfellow once said, "A single conversation across the table with a wise man is better than ten years' study of books." Whenever possible, get to know successful people. Find a way to engage them in conversation and learn what they know. It will expand your knowledge rapidly. Once expanded, a mind cannot return to its former size.

Character

As you create a change, there will be a few difficult moments. Success comes only to those who refuse to quit. To sustain yourself through this time of transformation, remember to keep motivating yourself. Staying focused on your vision will help maintain your motivation. Finally, keep a positive state of being, regardless of what is happening around you.

Communication

Whenever you communicate orally with anyone, most of your message is being transmitted through your body language and voice tone. Practice modulating your voice tone to be sure that your audience is getting your intended message. Maintain a positive state of being, and try to communicate your feelings. People love to be with and to do business with those who make them feel good.

Supporters

Select your friends and supporters carefully. Just as you influence them, they influence you.

As you transform yourself, the people around you tend to change. The ones who were benefiting from the "old" you may begin to alienate themselves from you. If they do not like where you seem to be going, they will often criticize or ridicule you. This is actually a good sign. It means that you are making a significant change in your life. However, if your growth and improvements really bother others, you may have to separate yourself, physically or mentally, from them.

Motivation of Others

What goes around, comes around. Motivate others whenever possible. Compliment them on their accomplishments. Appreciate any support they have extended. Then be ready to support them through their difficult times.

If you do this consistently, they will also be there for you. They will be more than willing to go the extra mile for you.

Synergy

If your vision is large enough, it is possible to go beyond teamwork. As more and more individuals become enthused with your vision, the ultimate state of teamwork can occur: the state of synergy. When this happens, everything becomes possible.

Balance

With piggybacking, you can get more out of twenty-four hours. Remember that life is really a psychological game. The game is either won or lost between your ears. Depending on how well you process your thoughts, you can really enjoy your life or just suffer through it. By controlling your mental processes, you can win the reward of a more balanced life.

Enjoyment

Life is like a concert. Nothing exists before the orchestra arrives. After the concert, the orchestra leaves and nothing remains. But between the time of the orchestra's arrival and departure, there is music.

How do you see the music of your life? Is it a full symphonic extravaganza, or is it one person playing the scales? Is it loud and blaring or quiet and soothing? Does it scare and hurt the people you touch in your life, or does it calm and support them? Is it dull and boring or exciting and invigorating? Does the audience enjoy the experience, or are they offended and upset?

You are the conductor of your life. You select the music and the various musicians. You can select and play any music you desire. Choose your music wisely, for the music the audience experiences is the same music you must live.

Appendix A
Estimated Time Spent On Each Major Activity

	Work	Relationships	Family	Fun and Play	Self-Improvement	Health	Sleep and Rest	Spiritual Development
6:00 a.m.								
6:15								
6:30								
6:45								
7:00								
7:15								
7:30								
7:45								
8:00								
8:15								
8:30								
8:45								
9:00								
9:15								
9:30								
9:45								
10:00								
10:15								
10:30								
10:45								
11:00								
11:15								
11:30								
11:45								

Appendix A
Estimated Time Spent On Each Major Activity

	Work	Relationships	Family	Fun and Play	Self-Improvement	Health	Sleep and Rest	Spiritual Development
12:00 p.m.								
12:15								
12:30								
12:45								
1:00								
1:15								
1:30								
1:45								
2:00								
2:15								
2:30								
2:45								
3:00								
3:15								
3:30								
3:45								
4:00								
4:15								
4:30								
4:45								
5:00								
5:15								
5:30								
5:45								

Appendix A
Estimated Time Spent On Each Major Activity

	Work	Relationships	Family	Fun and Play	Self-Improvement	Health	Sleep and Rest	Spiritual Development
6:00 p.m.								
6:15								
6:30								
6:45								
7:00								
7:15								
7:30								
7:45								
8:00								
8:15								
8:30								
8:45								
9:00								
9:15								
9:30								
9:45								
10:00								
10:15								
10:30								
10:45								
11:00								
11:15								
11:30								
11:45								

Appendix A
Estimated Time Spent On Each Major Activity

	Work	Relationships	Family	Fun and Play	Self-Improvement	Health	Sleep and Rest	Spiritual Development
12:00 a.m.								
12:15								
12:30								
12:45								
1:00								
1:15								
1:30								
1:45								
2:00								
2:15								
2:30								
2:45								
3:00								
3:15								
3:30								
3:45								
4:00								
4:15								
4:30								
4:45								
5:00								
5:15								
5:30								
5:45								

Index

Speeches and Seminars

Gary K. Yamamoto, Ph.D., founder and CEO of the Management and Sales Productivity Institute, is a professional speaker, seminar leader, consultant, and facilitator. In an environment of rapid change, Gary will demonstrate how to excel from the inside-out. Discover how to increase your performance and unleash your latent professional power in order to compete. Renew and re-energize yourself, and capitalize on all your abilities. Learn how to overcome your present mindset and limitations and create meaningful internal and external relationships with your customers, suppliers, and loved ones. The time to act is now!

An enthusiastic and energetic speaker, Gary's high-content, motivational presentations provide effective methods that can be easily applied for immediate results. He is a master at combining humor, story-telling, personal experiences and fun-filled audience interactions with his powerful message. You will leave his presentations feeling motivated, rejuvenated, and ready to transform yourself and your career!

Web page: http://www.wwim.com/speakers/samurai

Speeches and Seminars

Typical Topics:

- **Change**
- **Leadership**
- **Balance**
- **Professional Development**
- **Management**
- **Motivation**
- **Sales**
- **Personal Development**

Typical Titles:

The Future Belongs to Those Who Prepare For It!
Mastering Change
Developing Managers Into Leaders
Professional Power, Personal Excellence
Restore the Passion: For Work and For Life!
Balance and Energize Your Life!

To obtain more information on Gary's speeches, please contact:

Gold Stars Speakers Bureau
P.O. Box 37106, Tucson, AZ 85740-7106, U.S.A.
Phone: 520-742-4384, FAX: 520-797-3557
e-mail: 103473.3367@compuserve.com

Consultations

Dr. Gary Yamamoto is available for personal consultations. Here are a few of the consulting services provided by Dr. Yamamoto:

Transformational Management: Raising productivity is the primary role of managers. When you cannot hire the "right" people, Gary will help you create the "right" people by increasing individual performance and bottom-line productivity.

Total Quality Living: Personal excellence is attained through a balance of professional demands and personal desires. Gary will help you handle stress, energize your work, personally empower yourself, reinvent your career and your personal life, and restore excitement and zest into your life.

Mastering the Inner Game of Selling: In a highly competitive world where products and services appear very similar to consumers, selling requires more than simple product knowledge and closing techniques. Gary will help sales professionals perfect their inner state to become more effective at influencing customers, establishing relationships, and creating repeat sales.

Personal Development: Everyone desires to achieve professional excellence and success. To help you achieve your highest aspirations, Gary will assess your career path and assist you in developing a plan to guide you in attaining what you truly desire.

Retreats: Gary is also available for retreats. Away from the demands of work, Gary will provide seminars and one-on-one coaching. Gary will also facilitate management discussions to ensure that your management group receives the necessary skills to achieve its potential and increase organizational productivity.

To obtain more information on Dr. Yamamoto's consultations, please contact:

Gold Stars Speakers Bureau
P.O. Box 37106, Tucson, AZ 85740-7106, U.S.A.
Phone: 520-742-4384, FAX: 520-797-3557
e-mail: 103473.3367@compuserve.com

Ordering Information

Name: **(PLEASE PRINT)** ______________________________

Address: ______________________________

City: ____________________ State: _____ ZIP: __________

Phone: (day) (_____)______________ (evening) (_____)______________

Method of payment:

Auth: ______________
_____/_____/_____
for internal use only

☐ Check, U.S. funds

☐ Money order, U.S. funds, no cash please.

☐ Credit card: ☐ VISA ☐ Mastercard

Card # _____ - ________ - ________ - _______ Expiration date: ____/____/_____

Card Holder's Name: ______________________________

Authorized signature: ______________________________

Gift shipment? Message: ______________________________

____

Books - Resources for Successful Living	**Price**	**Qty**	**Total**
Professional Power, Personal Excellence (hdcvr)	$24.95		
Creative Dream Analysis (paperback)	$12.95		
		Subtotal	
		Tax (AZ residents add 7%)	
		Shipping & Handling	
		Total	

Shipping and handling for orders:

up to $20.00 - $3.50
$20.01- $50.00 - $4.00
$51.01-$100.00 - $4.50
over $100.00 - $5.00

- Calculate charges for each "ship to" address.
- If shipment to HI, AK, Puerto Rico or Canada, add $2.00 to above shipping charge.
- Foreign orders, please write/fax for prices.
- Most orders shipped by U.S. Postal Service, within 48 hours.

Mail order to:
Dynamic Pathways, Inc.
P.O. Box 37106
Tucson, AZ 85740-7106

or

Order by phone/fax:
Phone: 520-742-4384
FAX: 520-797-3557
Call toll free for orders only:
800-844-4384

Prices subject to change without notice. All sales final. Defective products will be replaced.

Thank you for your order!